Unhinged Habits

OTHER BOOKS BY JONATHAN GOODMAN

The Obvious Choice: Timeless Lessons on Success, Profit, and Finding Your Way

Ignite the Fire: The Secrets to a Successful Personal Training Career

Viralnomics: How to Get People to Want to Talk About You

THE WEALTHY FIT PRO'S GUIDES
Book 1: Starting Your Career

Book 2: Online Training (with Alex Cartmill)

Book 3: Getting Clients and Referrals (with Mike Doehla)

CHILDREN'S
Adventure, Adventure Awaits for Us All (with Alison Goodman)

Unhinged Habits

A Counterintuitive Guide for <u>**HUMANS**</u> to Have More by Doing Less

Jonathan Goodman

HarperCollins
Leadership

An Imprint of HarperCollins

Unhinged Habits
© 2026 by Jonathan Goodman

All rights reserved. No portion of this book may be reproduced, stored in a retrieval system, or transmitted in any form or by any means—electronic, mechanical, photocopy, recording, scanning, or other—except for brief quotations in critical reviews or articles, without the prior written permission of the publisher.

Published by HarperCollins Leadership, an imprint of HarperCollins Focus LLC, 501 Nelson Place, Nashville, TN 37214, USA.

Any internet addresses, phone numbers, or company or product information printed in this book are offered as a resource and are not intended in any way to be or to imply an endorsement by HarperCollins Leadership, nor does HarperCollins Leadership vouch for the existence, content, or services of these sites, phone numbers, companies, or products beyond the life of this book.

ISBN 978-1-4002-5345-6 (ePub)
ISBN 978-1-4002-5343-2 (HC)

Without limiting the exclusive rights of any author, contributor, or the publisher of this publication, any unauthorized use of this publication to train generative artificial intelligence (AI) technologies is expressly prohibited. HarperCollins also exercise their rights under Article 4(3) of the Digital Single Market Directive 2019/790 and expressly reserve this publication from the text and data mining exception.

HarperCollins Publishers, Macken House, 39/40 Mayor Street Upper, Dublin 1, D01 C9W8, Ireland (https://www.harpercollins.com)

Library of Congress Control Number: 2025947572

Art direction: Ron Huizinga
Cover design: Faceout Studio / Bret Hawkins
Interior Design: Neuwirth & Associates, Inc.

Printed in the United States of America
25 26 27 28 29 LBC 5 4 3 2 1

*For my miracle children: Calvin, Jaden, and Jasmine.
Let's never stop exploring together.*

THE 7 LAWS
OF INTENTIONAL LIFE DESIGN

Balance is for people afraid to burn for something.

You can have it all, just not all at once.

This is your call to reclaim the seasonality that your body and mind evolved to crave.

In a world designed to distract us, freedom can be obtained only through deliberate subtraction accomplished by following seven laws.

Law 1: Break free by seeking uncertainty, not by optimizing for comfort.
Escape from autopilot begins with exploration.

Law 2: Defeat hedonic adaptation through cycles of focus and renewal.
Beginnings hide themselves in ends.

Law 3: Embrace the humility of the unknown.
Shattering stale routines reveals rewarding new directions.

Law 4: Worthy struggle creates energy.
The easier your life becomes, the harder it feels.

Law 5: What you pursue has the power to either free you or quietly imprison you.
Beware of unchecked ambition.

Law 6: Prioritize social depth over breadth.
A few true friends outweigh countless weak connections.

Law 7: Grow separate to become stronger than the sum of your parts.
Championing differences forges the strongest relationships.

Integration: Freedom is found through deliberate subtraction.
You are not the author of your life, but you can be the editor.

CONTENTS

Introduction: The Secret Hidden in Plain Sight — xi

THE HALF-FULL CUP: SEPTEMBER 23, 2024 — 1

   1. Birds Never Sing in Caves — 7
   2. Define Your Season — 31
   3. Make More Mistakes — 65
   4. Choose Your Hard — 93

THE HALF-FULL CUP: OCTOBER 25, 2024 — 117

   5. The Paradox of Abundance — 123
   6. The Joy of Fewer Friends — 149
   7. Find Your Missing Half — 171
   8. The Profound Power of Ruthlessly Editing Your Life — 189

THE HALF-FULL CUP: NOVEMBER 2, 2024 — 215

Acknowledgments — 217
About the Author — 219

INTRODUCTION

The Secret Hidden in Plain Sight

Our lives have three priorities: money, health, and relationships. It's rare to have all three going well at the same time.

Young people often have relationships and health, but no money.

In midlife, we often have health and money, but no time for relationships.

When old, we're often rich in money and relationships, but poor in health.

I want you to achieve as much of the golden three at one time as possible.

The challenge we all face is balancing short-term desires with long-term planning. It's getting the order right—setting us up for a bright future without missing the magic in the present.

You should obviously get healthier to avoid getting sick, as opposed to frantically seeking cures after disease strikes. Or to grow love when you have it, so that it's there when you need it. But if there's no pain, there's no urgency.

It's the age-old problem of accountability. With a job, for example, accountability is external. With love and health, internal. External pressures always feel more urgent in the near term. And so, it's easy to excuse

Introduction

away personal things, only to face the magnitude of the mistake in our later years, once it's become too late.

Whether you've just finished college or decided not to go, own your company or work for one, have children or not, a simple self-examination is often all that is needed to recognize the disconnect between our actions and what we know, deep inside of us, is important.

Here's my promise to you:

By the end of this book, you'll have a practical framework to identify what truly matters in your life and the courage to eliminate everything else.

You'll learn how to break free from society's outdated expectations, your own bad habits, and the incessant pressure to do more.

Instead of constantly adding commitments, people, and things to your life, you'll become a master of the art of strategic subtraction—creating space for what's essential and discarding what's not.

And, throughout our journey together, I'll share a personal story that unfolded in real time as I wrote these pages. The universe, in its infinite dark humor, decided to test whether I actually lived this stuff.

This book is for you if:

- Your calendar's packed, yet you feel like you're missing what matters.

- You've bought things meant to bring happiness, but the satisfaction didn't last.

- You suspect you're living someone else's definition of success rather than your own.

- You're tired, unable to add more, yet there's still so much more you want to see and do.

You and I—humans—we're habitual by nature. Falling into patterns and getting stuck. Building habits and never questioning them. Digging ourselves into holes and digging, digging, digging, assuming that the way out is down so long as we dig faster or better or more efficiently—never noticing the ladder in our blind spot. Spinning frantically like gyroscopes, moving fast, yet never going anywhere. So driven to live successful lives that we settle for mediocre versions of them. Burned out by boreout.

Introduction

There's this water dispenser at home that my kids love to play with. They get a cup and fill it to the top. Then they add drops one by one, seeing how many they can place before the water finally spills over the edge.

The whole process is silly. An already full cup can maybe absorb a bit more, but you'll have to be careful, and it'll probably spill and make a mess anyway.

Alison and I get frustrated and toss them a towel. They clean up, and we wonder why they don't get it. Why they keep making the same mistake.

But then, one day, I realized that we adults do the same thing, don't we? We fill our cup to the brim with commitments and obligations. Then we try to add just a little bit more until it spills over.

Maybe we're the ones who don't get it.

You can't add more meetings into your color-coded calendar when the blocks already touch. Just as rubber bands snap when stretched beyond their limit and balloons burst when inflated beyond their capacity, your mental hard drive flashes red alerts of anxiety and forgotten promises when it's full.

Maybe we need a trash-cleaning function to remove 20 percent of the junk that we've allowed to accumulate. But we don't have one; our limbic system opposes it. Nine out of ten times it's better to remove than add. But our fear-loving brain remembers the one time we removed something that we needed, stopping us from doing it in the future.

And so we cover up the problem with to-do lists, productivity apps, and hacks, not because they're helpful but because they're easier in the short term. Temporary Band-Aids, blinding us to the reality that the more we add, the longer we wait to fix the core issue, and the bigger we let the problem get, the messier the puddle we're eventually going to have to clean up.

"The producer of old age is habit, the deathly process of doing the same thing in the same way at the same hour day after day, first from carelessness, then from inclination, at last from cowardice or inertia," wrote Edith Wharton, the first woman to win the Pulitzer Prize. That slaps.

This isn't theoretical for me. I'm a father of three who started as a personal trainer and ended up building companies generating $35M+ that have served more than two hundred thousand customers while traveling

Introduction

with my family to more than thirty countries. But more importantly, I've refused to accept the status quo—spending thirteen years challenging the societal norms of work, education, and lifestyle.

As a result, I've made a lot of mistakes.

I've burned out (many times) by prioritizing the wrong things, learning the hard way what really matters. I've missed family functions, and I've lost friends along the way too.

This is not a book summarizing academic research into happiness and fulfillment. You can find those elsewhere. I'm not a researcher. Rather, I'm an explorer, and I encourage you to be one as well.

Here's a bit of what's to come.

Chapter 1: Birds Never Sing in Caves gives you permission to break free from the noise of routine—to explore more and rediscover your true self.

Chapter 2: Define Your Season ditches the idea of "balanced progress" for strategic 8:4 seasons of intensity that will 5x your focus, 10x your output, and eliminate the guilt of not doing enough.

Chapter 3: Make More Mistakes is where you'll learn to leave your lazy assumptions behind.

Chapter 4: Choose Your Hard will show you how to discover revitalizing work worth doing.

Chapter 5: The Paradox of Abundance will help you escape the "when-I-finally" trap so that you enjoy life's special expiring moments, before it is too late.

Chapter 6: The Joy of Fewer Friends teaches the art of investing your time into a few enriching relationships so that you stop spreading your social life too thin.

Introduction

Chapter 7: Find Your Missing Half uncovers why lasting love isn't about finding your mirror image but growing apart, together—and how celebrating the journey transforms relationships.

Chapter 8: The Profound Power of Ruthlessly Editing Your Life reveals frameworks for strategic subtraction, ending our time together by helping you earn your freedom.

An unbalanced life well lived is an iterative process. A constant examination of yourself. Of your actions. Of what you own. And of who you surround yourself with.

We all know people who seek returns on investments they neglected to make. And I think we all fear becoming that person in our later years. The secret hidden in plain sight is to make prevention and preparedness pressing enough to act upon in the present.

Not wanting something is as good as not having it. The counterintuitive math of meaningful living is that less often equals more.

But even the best philosophy is empty if it has not been field tested on the battlefield of experience. Principles have value only if they save you when everything is burning down around you. The Instagram-friendly version of intentional living dies the moment that life punches you in the throat.

This book was forged in a fire. While writing it, something unexpected blindsided me, testing everything you're about to read. Let's start our story there.

Unhinged Habits

THE HALF-FULL CUP

September 23, 2024

There's a positive pregnancy test sitting on my desk.

Pregnancy is something I've gotten used to. By this point, Alison and I have had two boys and ten pregnancies.

Alison told me later that day that it feels different this time. She's in tune with her body. I guess that happens after so much loss. And emotion. And fluctuating hormones.

Then she felt ill. Really ill. Ill-to-the-point-of-not-being-able-to-stand-up-for-more-than-five-minutes-without-throwing-up ill.

On September 23, 2024, I sent my editor, Tim, an email:

Writing is going well.

But my wife is extremely sick right now. She's been in bed for three days. It's nothing to worry about. She's pregnant. But it's early. We aren't telling anybody.

What this also means though is that there's a good chance it'll be like this for a while. Weeks, or even months.

I'm only telling you this because I want to ask well in advance for a potential extension for the *Habits* manuscript delivery.

I didn't think much of it at the time, but looking back, I see how deeply ingrained this instinct was—this automatic response to push through, to keep going, to act as if things were normal even when they weren't. I had spent years operating under this pattern, so I didn't even question it. But maybe I should have.

Routines. Patterns. *Habits.* They're the invisible architects of our lives. Some serve us well. Others trap us in downward cycles we don't even recognize we're caught in.

Earlier that year, nighttime after a flight.

We arrived home after four months in Nicaragua and Mexico. The kids are playing, happy to see their toys again. Alison and I go upstairs to put our backpacks down.

We walk into our bedroom and start laughing.

Our bed has four pillars. Over a year ago, Calvin made a giant spiderweb across the top of it with Alison's yarn. In the middle of the web, hanging down, I kid you not, is a Slinky.

That thing hung there for a year. My wife and I slept under a spiderweb that caught a Slinky *for over a year*. It was cute when Calvin did that when he was five. He'll be seven in a week. Maybe it shouldn't exist anymore.

It's easy to fall into patterns. To lazily accept even the silliest additions to our lives. To never reassess whether a thing helps us, hurts us, takes up space, or in this case, makes any freaking sense. To keep things how they are because that's how they were.

How much stuff exists in your home or life that any outsider would tell you needs to go?

How many things are you currently doing that you don't need to do but have always done and so you mindlessly keep doing it?

What is it in your life that's "just there," that no longer needs to be there?

I call this the Slinky Effect—when we get so used to the silly invisible habits running our lives that we don't even notice them anymore. These "Slinkys" accumulate in our careers, relationships, possessions, and daily routines until we're living lives we didn't consciously choose.

And that's the problem.

In a modern world designed to distract us, we don't actively architect our lives. We default into them.

Most people think the solution to feeling overwhelmed is to do more, optimize better, and work harder. That's wrong. This book will show you how to do less, but with more intention.

When you're done reading it, you'll walk downstairs, get a pair of scissors, and cut that damn Slinky-eatin' spiderweb off your bed.

My last book, *The Obvious Choice*, ended with this story:

> It's 5:00 a.m. I'm working in the empty lobby of a hotel in the Dominican Republic.
>
> A man stumbled past. Vodka, maybe some rum. He looked at me and said: "That's sad, dude. You're on vacation." At that moment, all I could think about was that I never wanted to once again live a life where I had to go on vacation to escape.
>
> "*¿Dónde puedo conseguir un café con azúcar por favor?*"
>
> I asked the lobby attendant in my cave-man Spanish where I could get a coffee. He told me I was too early and would have to wait thirty minutes.

In that book, I shared lessons about business and success that helped me find my way professionally after I strayed off course. That took me from lost and aimless to being so excited for my work that I was too early for coffee.

The Obvious Choice was a business book. I like money. It's important. But there's more to life than profit. And so consider this the other half of the story.

Just before I clicked send on the email to my editor, Tim, asking for an extension, I added this:

> There's actually a few through lines with "Habits" depending on how things play out with Alison's pregnancy-induced illness that might be a powerful story to tell, maybe in the epilogue. Or, as an interlude.

Themes of resiliency: If my cup was full, this would have tipped me over. Now it's a challenge, nothing more.

Themes of physical strength: Years of showing up to the gym when I didn't feel like it banked me a lot of fitness in reserve.

Themes of family and community: Our decision to live close to my parents and investments into building incredible relationships with neighbors has provided me with support when it was needed the most.

I've no idea what's going to happen or how this will pan out. But I'll take notes and try to make reflections ongoing. Then, when this period passes, I'll write it up and maybe we can add it into the book somehow.

Overworking is a modern vice. Being busy is an excuse for not taking care of yourself or the people that matter to you.

You don't get less busy by working harder. Ridiculous. That's like trying to stop a storm with more wind. You get less busy by doing fewer things but doing them better and with more intentionality.

In Toronto, the streets are noisy with cars, chaotic with frenetic energy. Everyone's always rushing somewhere. But that's the noise of laziness and fatigue, not activity. As G. K. Chesterton wrote, "It's the happy man who does the useless things; the sick man isn't strong enough to be idle." If everyone walked, the streets in Toronto would be quieter but more alive. You only own your time if you can afford to waste it.

If your days are full yet not fulfilling, it's time for you to examine your life honestly and, perhaps, break some bad habits.

This feels like a good starting point. Let's start exploring.

1.

Birds Never Sing in Caves

*Break free by seeking uncertainty,
not by optimizing comfort.*

No matter how deep down the achievement rabbit hole you are, it's possible to dig your way out—to walk about wide-eyed like a kindergartner, excited once again about the littlest blade of grass, days filled with surprises.

Thoreau wrote, "Birds do not sing in caves." And neither do we. When you explore with intention, you cease to become intent in your complacency.

Exploration isn't about geographic distance but about the internal journey of breaking free from the caves of our own making—those comfortable, predictable routines that dull our senses and shrink our world.

There's this cliché that says you've got two choices for how to live your life. One is as though nothing is a miracle. The other is as though everything is a miracle. A parking spot opening up at Costco, right near the entrance. Your phone not autocorrecting to "duck." Getting through an entire video call without anybody asking "Can you hear me now?"

The worst thing about clichés is that they mean nothing—right up until the moment they mean everything.

The best cup of coffee I ever had was made from a packet of Folgers instant in a cheap yellow plastic cup, the kind they give toddlers at parties.

Unhinged Habits

It was day six of a four-day trip to Ometepe, an island in Nicaragua made up of two volcanoes. We got stranded there. High winds. The ferry couldn't return.

Scrambling, we found a new place to stay. Across the road, a bamboo shack served food to local workers.

The woman who ran the joint had that aged, tanned, and wrinkled skin that made you not sure whether she was fifty or ninety years old. Told us that she'd been there for forty years. Has six kids working construction in Costa Rica. When asked if she has a husband, she laughed and said, "*Algunos.*" A few.

No menu. *Desayuno* was eighty córdoba (~$2.10 USD): two overcooked eggs, rice, beans, and fried plantain.

We were lost. Stranded in the middle of nowhere.

My wife was sitting beside me, and Bee, our nanny, beside us. My freshly tattooed mother-in-law was looking for treasures among the rocks with my two boys. And I was gazing out at Lake Nicaragua, fully alive, wondering how in the hell we all got here, drinking the best damn coffee of my life.

Maps, assistants, and googling everything diminish the magic. In many ways, the worst thing that can happen is that things go to plan.

Travel is for turning on; vacations are for shutting off. Travel heightens your senses; vacations dull them. Travel's for discovery; vacation, escapism. Vacations are fine. Designing a daily life that you don't need to escape from, however, is better.

This chapter has a lot of examples from far-flung places. Some stories are a little crazy. But I'm not going to use the "t" word. That's because you don't have to get on an airplane (or even leave your home) to make day-to-day life more fun and exciting. Instead, I'll use the word *exploration*.

First, permission to not do it all.

Then, the Explorer's Compass framework to safely introduce much-needed unpredictability back into your life.

And finally, we'll shake off the shackles of your limitations.

It's time for you to escape autopilot.

BRAILLING THE WORLD

Crater Lake was circled on our map because all national parks and monuments were circled on our map.

Alison and I parked at the same time as another family. Before they stepped out of their car, both parents bent over their phones. "It should be this way," the dad said, as he pointed in the direction of the visitor center.

I smiled without showing my teeth to the man and nodded my head slightly, the way awkward guys say hello to one another, and we followed their family up the path.

Some natural spectacles take your breath away with their sheer power. The Grand Canyon in Arizona, the Nā Pali Coast in Kauai, or the jagged edges of the Rocky Mountains that flank you as you drive from Banff to Jasper in Alberta.

Others, like Crater Lake, are so deceptively plain that they give you breath. Like, how is something so perfect in its simplicity possible here on this rough earth. That the only explanation involves the existence of a higher power—an artist—who long ago chose this spot to be her canvas, taking a paintbrush for each of our senses. The smell of the pines, the sound of the wind, the sight of the teal blue water, the feel of the dirt path under your feet, and the taste of the peanut butter and jelly mixing in your mouth as you take it all in.

"Beautiful," said the mom from the family in the parking lot. "It looks just like the picture."

It looks just like the picture. Is there a sadder phrase in all the English language? To be so well prepared. So organized. So afraid of the unknown. To be in so much of a rush that you stop brailling the world like a toddler seeing his first tree.

When I asked my friend how his honeymoon went, he said that it flew by. That he's exhausted. That over the course of two weeks in Thailand, they stayed in six different places. "We'd both been looking forward to this trip for so long and overscheduled ourselves," he told me.

Unhinged Habits

A few pieces of advice for you to add more wonder into your experiences.

Don't look it up in advance. Photoshopped images of what you're about to see ruin what you're about to see.

Don't do your research. Learning about the thing *while you're visiting the thing* adds to the joy of the thing.

Don't move on too quickly. You'll miss out on more than you see regardless, so you may as well really see what you're there to see.

Accept that no matter what you do, or how much you do, you won't do it all. You won't even do very much. So don't try. Instead, linger. Take your time. Smell the flowers. Touch the tree bark. Eat prosciutto with the locals. Listen to the birds. And maybe even play a game of freeze tag. Then, as the sun sets, shut up and watch.

One time I was on a plane from Toronto to Los Angeles. There were stronger headwinds than expected. We made an emergency landing somewhere in the north of Mexico to refuel.

A Japanese guy was sitting beside me. He didn't speak English well. As a result, he didn't understand the overhead announcements and thought that we'd arrived at LAX.

I explained to him that we were actually in Mexico for more gas.

He nodded, took out a notebook, flipped to a page that said Mexico and put a checkmark beside it. Been there, done that. Guess he never has to go back.

Which is sad. Because Mexico is special.

The colors. Oh my goodness, the colors in Mexico. And the music. The food. Real Mexican food. Not Taco Tuesday at Tiago's Taqueria at the corner of W. Eighteenth and Morgan. And the energy. The *vibrancy*.

Oh, and the people. One time our family was waiting to eat. Calvin was three. A local boy was having a birthday party down an alleyway. We hear a voice. "*Para ti,*" the boy said as he handed Calvin a loot bag before running back to his party.

Mexico is special. But you've gotta be there to know that. Like, really be there. Not sit on a plane on a tarmac for thirty minutes. Not go to an all-inclusive resort.

Checking off that you've visited a place doesn't mean that you've been to that place.

Off the coast of Newfoundland in Canada there are two self-governing French islands called Saint Pierre and Miquelon. It's France. They use Euros. Bake baguettes. The whole thing. A political remnant of a bygone era. Dave Ruel grew up there. He invited me to visit for a week of lobster trapping, cod fishing, and wine drinking.

I met a passport stamp collector on the flight over. Apparently that's a thing. Her plan was to clear customs, get the unique passport stamp, stay overnight in a hotel, and fly home the following day.

To each their own.

But my unsolicited advice to her is to consider staying an extra night or two. Maybe, you know, check out the place. Mosey about. Grab a latte. Eat some cheese. Learn about how Al Capone took advantage of the unique political makeup and location of the archipelago as a hub for bootlegging alcohol during the Prohibition era. Might be fun.

The paradox of trying to fit it all in is that the only way to experience more is to schedule less.

Maps and guidebooks have checklists; life doesn't.

More focus on the doing, less on the done, I say.

BAND-AIDS IN URUGUAY

There's a quip about a Buddhist monk that I like.

"Where are you going?" A man asks the monk.

"Ask my horse," the monk replies.

Getting lost seems like the beginning of finding your way. Or finding another way. "Let go or be dragged," states the Zen proverb.

It's hard to know where a bus will take you in Montevideo, the capital city of Uruguay.

Street names stretch long and, because they commemorate dates, people, or events, many resemble each other. The map we had condensed the names to fit. All that we would see, for example, would be *Avenida Genera . . .*

Unhinged Habits

Okay, so a general. We're looking for a general. Right. Probably. Which general are we looking for? Flores, Pagola, Enrique Martínez. Maybe General Flores y Garibaldi.

At home, in comfort, I go on autopilot. Sometimes, at the end of the day, in that time when time slows down after dinner but before bed, I think about my day. Try to remember what I did.

And I can't think of anything . . .

That's because I wasn't there. Well, I was there, obviously, but not *there*. You know what I mean. I was gliding. A leaf floating down a stream. Detached and passive, being bounced around with a sense of direction but without full engagement.

Being more present leads to less stress, fewer negative thoughts, more focus, improved happiness, and better control of our emotions. Cool, I buy that. How do you actually be present? Meditation's one way. I've never been able to meditate. Getting lost is another.

One day we were on a bus rolling along Avenida 18 de Julio when a man got on—thick black hair with a bit of a gut; a buttoned-up plaid blue shirt tucked into his jeans; gray backpack slung over one shoulder. He walked past the driver without paying.

"*Trita. Trita,*" he said, holding a box of Band-Aids.

Really dude. Band-Aids. You know, in America they sell chocolate bars on the bus. And I've got a hankering for a Mars bar.

A woman waved him over. She gave him a coin. He gave her a Band-Aid. Then another. And another. He made four sales. Exited the bus. Walked across the street. And waited for one going in the opposite direction.

Trita-Man reminded me of a sales lesson I'd long since forgotten.

The legendary advertising man Gary Halbert once asked a room of aspiring copywriters a question:

"Imagine you're opening a hamburger stand on the beach—what do you need most to succeed?"

"Location," one said. "Taste," said another.

"You both missed the most important thing. What you need most is a starving crowd," Halbert responded.

Many of the women riding that bus in Uruguay wore thin heels. Montevideo's full of old cobblestone streets. By the end of the day, they had blistered feet.

Our hero went to the *farmacia*, bought a box of Band-Aids, hopped a bus, and sold it to them: a starving crowd.

You notice things when you explore. When you allow yourself to be lost, you invite your system to go on high alert. Reading every street sign. Eyes forward, not down and locked into a device tracking your exact position via a blue dot on a screen.

SAFETY THIRD

When you explore with intention, as we've discussed, you break free from those caves of comfortable routine. This applies whether you're navigating unfamiliar cobblestone streets in Montevideo or simply breaking patterns closer to home. But stepping outside our routines requires overcoming a powerful human instinct: the desire for safety and predictability.

My best friend was in a rut. I'll call him Andrew. He'd gotten a master's degree and a good-paying job. But Andrew was bored. And Andrew was lonely. Every day was the same: go to the job site, manage unmanageable contractors, go home, make dinner, watch Netflix, and go to sleep.

"It's my month of yes," he told me over the phone.

"What?" I said.

"I'm bored, man. And I need a girl. For thirty days, I'm going to say yes to everything. If somebody asks me to do something, I'll go. If I see a flyer for something that looks remotely interesting, I'll sign up and show up."

What Andrew was doing—though I didn't have the language for it at the time—was exactly what we've been discussing: getting out of his own way, breaking his routine, and exploring his own world. He had developed comfortable habits that weren't serving him and was aware enough to know that the longer he waited to do something about it, the harder it would be to escape.

This is the explorer's dilemma in everyday life.

Just as brailling the world requires letting go of maps and expectations, breaking free from our routines requires deliberately introducing

Unhinged Habits

uncertainty. Andrew was placing himself in situations where he'd need to be fully present. Where he couldn't operate on autopilot.

Near the end of the month he invited me to a vodka bar called Proof. Now this might surprise you, but I am not the type of guy that frequents vodka bars with single word names. For him, I said I'd put on pants, lace up my three-stripe Adidas, and roll out.

We get there and he meets this girl: Amy; a friend of a friend. They hit it off.

It's nearing the end of the night now. Andrew and I are hanging with our other friend Chris, trying to look as suave as any three dudes can look huddled together just before closing, sipping vodka drinks through tiny straws that only the boldest explorers like us drink from to satisfy our parched throats. Amy walks over, says her friends are leaving, and exchanges numbers with Andrew before walking away.

A minute passes. Two minutes pass. I bump my top lip with my straw; miss my mouth. Smile. Hope nobody noticed. Of course nobody noticed. Then, out of nowhere, Andrew says, "Screw it. Month of yes." And takes off.

Soon after, Chris mutters under his breath, "He brought her back." Then he yells it and points at the door. "HE BROUGHT HER BACK!"

They're married now, Andrew and Amy.

But Andrew's story of transformation was just beginning—one that would ultimately test whether he could apply the same courage to his career as he had to his love life. You'll meet Andrew a few more times. First, when I speak about true friendship in chapter 6 and then again in chapter 8, when he finds his freedom over a decade later.

His story illustrates something profound about exploration: it often means ranking safety third. Not first, not even second, but third—behind growth and experience. This doesn't mean being reckless. It means recognizing that avoiding all risk is itself the greatest risk.

As the author Cory Muscara puts it: "If you want to be safe, don't do anything. Don't go out, drive, experiment, learn, try. Nothing. Then you'll be safe. And one day, you'll still die."

Too much comfort results in a false state of confidence, dulling your senses—the same senses that come alive when you're lost in Montevideo or you're putting yourself out there, trying to meet the girl of your dreams. When everything is predictable, we shut off.

You don't need to go to far-flung places (though I highly recommend it) and do things like get marooned on remote islands in Nicaragua (though it is fun) or figure out the bus system in Uruguay (though I wouldn't stop you). Start small. Find little ways close to home that, stealing a phrase from the poet Rumi, "purchase bewilderment."

When somebody tells me that their life is boring, I tell them to "go ahead, be boring."

If by boring you mean doing things like folding the laundry while listening to podcasts on history or mathematics or chemical engineering, then keep doing that. If you mean walking the dusty stacks at used book stores, or going for coffee with friends, or visiting museums and reading the placards about long-gone civilizations, or touring galleries and staring at paintings by long-dead artists, or attending antique car auctions without ever bidding, or collecting vinyl records, or baseball cards, action figures, comics, pins, buttons, old Nintendo games, novelty salt and pepper shakers . . . All of this is fine too.

But . . . if by boring you mean that you have no interests. That you never seek out new knowledge or learn new skills. Or that you lack a passion for even the most random, useless, and otherwise uninteresting things like learning to speak Klingon or becoming the worldwide *Wizard of Oz* trivia champion. That all you do is sit and scroll. Then yeah, that's a problem. You should stop doing nothing and start doing something. Even if it's a boring hobby. Because at least it's your boring hobby.

It's okay to be boring. But it's not okay to be vacant.

When a plane takes off, you feel its movement. But when it's in the air, even when the speed is nearly four times the speed of takeoff, you don't feel the movement of the plane. When it's time for the plane to land, when it's decelerating, you feel the movement again.

That's because our body and mind feel changes in speed, not speed itself.

You're only boring if you *yourself* think that you're uninteresting. To be less boring, be less boring to yourself. Let others think what they may.

Unhinged Habits

Rank safety third. Don't abandon caution, but recognize that your greatest moment of growth and joy will come from taking calculated risks. From forcing yourself to navigate uncertainty with intention rather than shriveling up with fear. When you approach life this way, you'll discover that exploration isn't just about going to new places but about becoming more fully alive wherever you are.

Here's a few ways to start exploring locally.

Eat at that weird ethnic restaurant on the corner. Don't look at the menu. Ask what they like, eat what they give you, and drink what they bring you. If it's nasty, no big deal. Get a bucket of fried chicken on your way home.

Be a tourist in your own city. Go to a random pocket of your town. Wander without your phone, not knowing what you'll do, where you'll eat, or whom you'll meet.

Discover new books. Choose a major award for books: Pulitzer, Man Booker, Hugo, whatever. Then find the winners and runners-up from a random year. Say, 1998. Download a sample from each on your Kindle or reserve them from the library. Sample each and continue to read when one grabs you.

Each of these seemingly small adventures retrains your brain to embrace uncertainty rather than fear it. Like the Band-Aid seller on the Montevideo bus, you'll begin to see opportunities where others see only risk. You'll develop your awareness, your adaptability, and your openness to the unexpected.

LAWS OF LIVING LOST

The author A. J. Jacobs once tried to thank every person responsible for his morning cup of coffee. He gave up at a thousand. There's more complexity in even the littlest things in our world than our brains can comprehend.

You don't know much more than you know. Admit it, you're lost. Bumbling about in the fun house, bamboozled by the wall of mirrors. Like a stray cat roaming the alleys, seeking warmth and familiarity in places that feel foreign.

The sidewalk you walk on. Did you know that it's reinforced with rebar? Or that concrete strengthens with compression and weakens with stretch? Have you ever thought about the logistic complexity of the billion-or-so wooden pallets that were used to transport everything, in every home, basically, everywhere?

Accept that you'll get lost. Accept that you're already lost. Explore. Try stuff. Because the more that you try stuff, the more you'll be forced to figure it out. And the more you figure it out, the more confidence you'll gain in your ability to *figure it out*. Eventually, you'll learn that everything is figureoutable. That's when life gets real fun.

Exploration is not just about going to new places but is a profound process of identity reconstruction. Each time we step outside our comfort zone, we're not merely collecting experiences—we're actively rewriting our internal narrative.

When you allow yourself to become temporarily "lost"—whether in a foreign city, a new skill, or an unfamiliar social context—you suspend the rigid definitions of who you believe yourself to be. You become malleable. Adaptable. Your sense of self is no longer a fixed point but a fluid landscape of potential.

This is why travelers often return home slightly changed. Why hobbyists who dive deep into new crafts speak of transformation. You are not discovering a new version of yourself; you are actively creating one with each uncertain step.

The most powerful exploration doesn't happen in the world around you. It happens in the world within you.

Being lost is an inevitable reality of being a human being. Never knowing exactly where you are or how things work or what you're doing is normal. Be proud of it. Shout it out. "*I am lost!*"

Acceptance is the first step. Next, how to live in a perpetually lost state. Or reality.

Think about early mountaineers like Hugh Stutfield or Herman Wooley traversing the Columbia Icefield. We now know it's 230 square kilometers. They didn't. Early explorers didn't know whether they'd be in the wilderness for a few days or a few months. They carried their supplies on their backs. They didn't have a map because they were the ones *making the map*.

Unhinged Habits

"Early explorers never expected to know exactly where they were," wrote Rebecca Solnit in *A Field Guide to Getting Lost*. "Yet, at the same time, many of them knew their instruments pretty well and understood their trajectories within a reasonable degree of accuracy."

Ah, that's it: The two laws of living lost:

1. Know your instruments.
2. Maintain the correct general trajectory.

On the Pacific coast of Mexico about forty minutes north of Puerto Vallarta there's a hike called Monkey Mountain. You can choose between the south or north trail.

The south trail isn't hard. It's well marked; basically a service road. Most people who do it sweat, get to the top, walk down, and take an air-conditioned shuttle back to town. Takes a few hours. Check, check. Been there, done that. Got pics for social media.

The north trail, on the other hand, isn't well marked.

Our taxi driver dropped my wife, six-year old son, and me off in the middle of nowhere. No signs. No people. After walking for twenty minutes we saw a farmer. *¿Mono montaña?* we asked. He pointed back to where we came.

Equip yourself by learning a few phrases. Translation apps have made that easy for travel. It's no different when exploring a new hobby. For example, if you wanted to explore CrossFit, learn some jargon. Knowing what Rx and WOD means helps keep first-day jitters at bay. Language is an instrument.

Along the way, we passed more farms. Dogs barked. I grabbed a stick. They left us alone. Karate senseis don't teach how to start fights; they teach how to avoid them. Self-control comes from conflict avoidance, the de-escalation of aggression. Physically weak people are generally timid. As a result, they miss out on a lot. Physical preparedness is an instrument.

We saw a father and son bouldering along the way with a guide. They weren't going up the mountain. Instead, they were messing about for a few hours on a random boulder in the jungle. "Whenever we go on vacation, we try to find a place to climb," the dad said.

What a wonderful way to waste time.

Alison and Calvin joined them for a while before moving on. Knowing your trajectory gives you the confidence to go with the flow and veer off the path.

At one point, we lost the trail. My wife and son stopped. I bushwhacked to a higher point. Cut up my legs. Was bleeding. From the high point, I could make out the trail. I shouted to Alison. She led Calvin. Then I climbed back down and joined them. Sometimes you have to double back, walk extra. Getting lost burns more calories. Physical endurance is an instrument.

Ticks latched onto me when I went off-trail. We carefully removed them. Disinfected my skin with alcohol. Did full-body tick checks on all our bodies after the hike. Monitored to make sure I didn't develop a fever the next few days. Basic first aid is an instrument.

We got to the top.

"Where did you come from?" another hiker asked.

I told him.

"Oh, I heard that way is dangerous," he said.

It wasn't really. The hike took us longer. We got lost a few times. We have a few scrapes and cuts. But we knew our general direction and trusted our instruments. I didn't say that to them. That would've been weird. If I'm honest, I wasn't all that interested in a conversation. Was looking forward to my sandwich. All that I said was, "Yeah. Kinda dangerous."

At the bottom again now. We tried to call a cab. No luck. The three of us are stranded.

We finally saw a car. One of those mini delivery trucks. White. The back carriage was clearly handmade. Wood splintering. A few planks across but no roof. He would have been delivering produce (probably watermelons) and was on his way home in the opposite direction of where we needed to go.

Alison waved him down. Explained our situation in broken Spanish. He motioned for us to get in the back. Said he'd drop us off in town.

The tailgate hinge was busted. We had to climb up and over to get in. Alison went first. I lifted Calvin. Then I got in. We all stood in the back, knees bent, holding on to a wooden plank.

Unhinged Habits

The man drove fast. The carriage we were in bounced on every divot and root.

"This is dangerous, right?" Calvin asked.

Yeah, buddy. It is. But, like, a good kind of danger. The kind of danger that really isn't that dangerous. Where you know you'll be okay. The kind of danger that makes the hair on your arms stick up and your knees shake. Where the wind stings your eyes, but you just let it happen because you have more important things to focus on. You're alert. In tune. On guard. Aware of everything. The kind of danger where your mind can't wander. Where you forget about all the nagging annoyances in your life. Where you have no other choice than to focus on what's happening right here, right now. The kind of danger that makes you feel 100 percent alive.

There's a saying that life is short. And I believe that to be true. But it's deeper than that. Each moment you have just disappears. If you're not present for it. If you're stressed out or you're anxious or you're thinking about something else, you missed it.

There's a sweet spot of enjoyment. Of novelty, complexity, and challenge—of adventure—to seek. "Somewhere between boringly easy and frustratingly incomprehensible is a satisfying midrange of uncertainty that you can grapple with productively," wrote Alex Hutchinson in *The Explorer's Gene*.

The rewards we get from doing difficult things seem extra sweet because of the sharp contrast between the unpleasantness of the experience and the joy of achievement. Effort, according to research in *Trends in Cognitive Sciences*, is both costly and valued.

"We're not interested in having no error," Alex continued. "We're looking for digestible errors—gaps in our knowledge that we can efficiently fill."

WHERE CHALLENGE MEETS ENJOYMENT

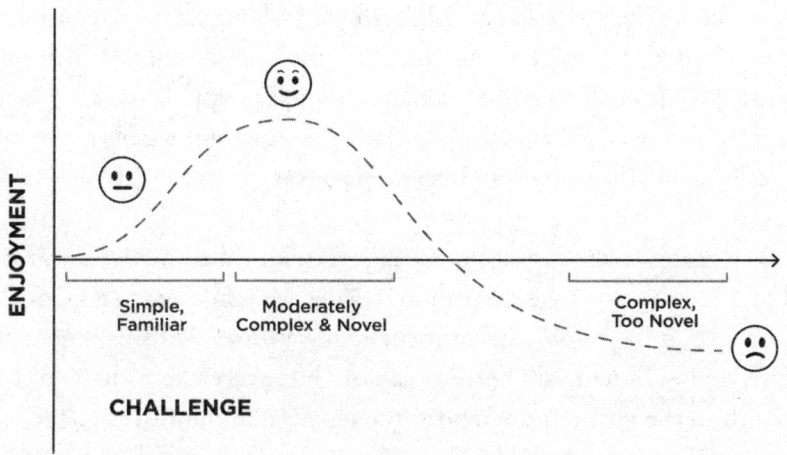

Finding your optimal challenge zone is key to meaningful growth. The Wundt Curve shows us that we thrive in that middle space—where activities aren't boring but aren't overwhelming either. Push your boundaries gradually, and your comfort with uncertainty will expand. When you operate in this sweet spot, exploration becomes exhilarating rather than exhausting. (©Unhinged Habits)

Uncertainty isn't motivating. What's motivating is the perception of reducing uncertainty. Of reducing prediction error. Of figuring something out. For all of us, there is such a thing as an optimal challenge. One that's neither too easy nor too hard at any given time.

Humans don't actually pursue happiness; we pursue only relief from uncertainty. Happiness emerges momentarily as a byproduct whenever uncertainty briefly disappears.

I have plenty of friends who say, "Well, exploring is for you, not everyone. I'm not much of an explorer myself." What this means is that they have no desire to find their way up the back of a mountain along an unmarked trail in Mexico. But that doesn't mean that they aren't exploring in other ways.

As you explore more, you earn confidence. Your challenge line moves. And you'll crave more novel experiences. This explains why people who travel a lot tend to opt for more obscure locales. It's no different from music aficionados preferring more complex sounds over time.

The watermelon farmer dropped us off in a town called Higuera Blanca.

Unhinged Habits

Calvin bought a gross marshmallow pastry at a bodega. Alison and I got water and cookies. Then we walked to the town square and grabbed a cab.

Confidence lags experience. Modern life is sheltered, temperature controlled, overfed, and underchallenged. It's too comfortable. Which makes us fearful. Our challenge line stagnates, which paralyzes us into inaction over time—even the smallest unpredictable or uncomfortable event seems colossal. Asking the waiter for extra ketchup should not make your armpits sweat.

In the long term, exploring, in aggregate, leads to discovery, growth, and joy. So why don't we do it more? James March, a management theorist, believes it has to do with immediate reward mechanisms ingrained in our society: "Humans are born to explore but everywhere chained by the demands of the next annual report, the next election, or the need to avoid inconvenient gaps on their CV."

What if uncertainty isn't something to fear but a resource to be cultivated? An exploration mindset is less about having all the answers and more about becoming comfortable with not knowing. A few reframes:

- **Uncertainty is an opportunity.** The unexpected isn't a threat. It's an invitation to discover something new about yourself.
- **Prolonged comfort is dangerous.** Stagnation grows moss.
- **Failure is information.** Instead of letting it get you down, consider what you learned to avoid or what you will do differently next time.
- **Flexible intentions are better than rigid expectations.** Set adaptive goals. View your path as a compass, not a GPS.
- **"I wonder what I might discover" is more useful than "I already know."** Cultivate radical curiosity.
- **Ask naive questions and drop preconceptions.** Set your ego aside and embrace a beginner's mindset.

Despite the long-term benefits, we don't explore as much as we should. Instead, we exploit too much of what we already know. That's because exploiting is predictable and proximate in contrast to exploring, which is distant, uncertain, and often negative in the short term.

If all this is motivating you to get there more, here's a helpful tool for intentional, safe, exploration.

THE EXPLORER'S COMPASS

Modern life often chains us to predictability, but exploration doesn't require scaling unmapped mountains. It starts with a simple framework I call the Explorer's Compass—a guide for intentionally introducing uncertainty into your life.

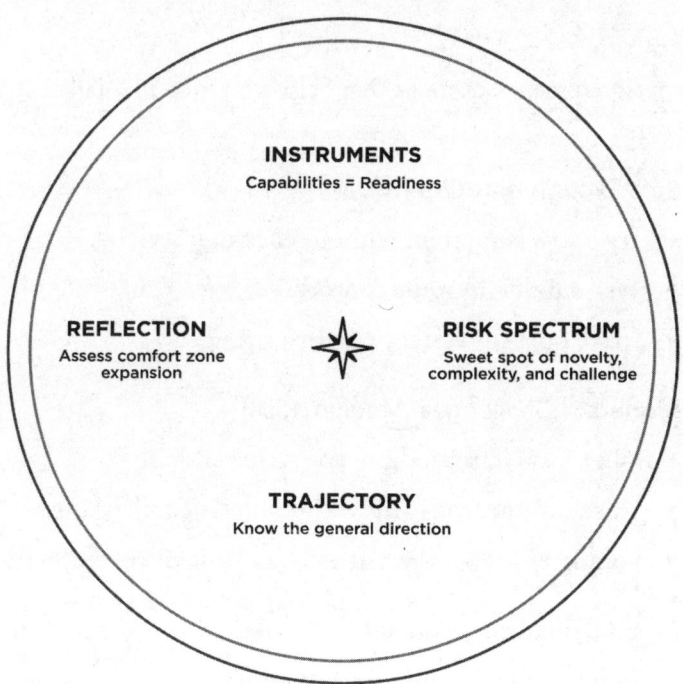

The four tools to safely introduce meaningful uncertainty in everyday life, so that you expand your capabilities and confidence. (©Unhinged Habits)

Instruments

Just like early mountaineers carried essential tools, you need personal instruments. These aren't physical objects but capabilities:

Unhinged Habits

- **Language:** Learn three to five key phrases in a new domain. Want to explore photography? Learn a few key technical terms. Interested in cooking? Culinary jargon.
- **Physical Preparedness:** Build basic skills that increase confidence. This might mean taking a self-defense class, improving basic first aid knowledge, or developing moderate physical fitness.
- **Mental Tool Kit:** Cultivate adaptability through small, intentional challenges that make you uncomfortable. Like requesting a 10 percent discount on your coffee or asking a stranger for directions on the street.

Risk Spectrum

Create a personal risk assessment that helps you incrementally expand your comfort zone:

1. **Safe Experiments (Low Risk)**
    - Try a new restaurant without checking reviews.
    - Take a different route to work.
    - Strike up a conversation with a stranger.

2. **Moderate Challenges (Medium Risk)**
    - Join a class in something you've never done.
    - Travel to a nearby town without detailed planning.
    - Volunteer for a project at work outside of your expertise.

3. **Bold Adventures (High Risk)**
    - Solo travel to an unfamiliar country.
    - Start a side hustle in a new industry.
    - Commit to give a public talk.

Trajectory

Exploration isn't about having a perfect map but about understanding your general direction. This means:

- Setting loose, flexible goals instead of rigid plans.
- Remaining open to unexpected detours.

Reflection

After a bout of exploration (big or small), take fifteen minutes and ask yourself three questions:

1. What unexpected thing did I learn about myself?
2. How did I just introduce meaningful uncertainty?
3. In what way did my comfort zone just expand?

Remember: the goal isn't constant upheaval but a sustained openness to the unknown. Exploration is less about the external journey and more about your internal willingness to be surprised.

And finally, some self-reflection for you to do right now:

When was the last time I intentionally did something that made me uncomfortable?

_____
_____
_____
_____

What story am I telling myself about why I can't explore?

_____
_____
_____
_____

Unhinged Habits

Where in my life have I mistaken familiarity for safety?
_____
_____
_____
_____

What would I attempt if failure was guaranteed to teach me something valuable?
_____
_____
_____
_____

You can download the Explorer's Compass worksheet to help you safely expand your comfort zone at www.Jonathangoodman.com/explore.

SHAKE OFF YOUR SHACKLES

"You told the waiter I was pregnant!?"

I finished writing my last book overlooking the Pacific Ocean from a luxury hotel. Most days, I had the place to myself.

Where I wrote, coffee cost sixty Mexican pesos (about three dollars) and came with a free refill. René knew exactly how I like it (black, with honey). After four months, it was time to leave. I said goodbye and told him that I'd be back next year but wasn't sure when because Alison was pregnant.

We slapped hands and bro hugged (two back pats). I said thank you for taking care of me. And meant it. And that was it.

Alison ended up losing the baby. It was our sixth miscarriage. By then, we had learned to wait a while before sharing the news. But I had to tell somebody. And so, I told René. My parents never knew about the pregnancy. Neither did my best friend. The only person who knew Alison was pregnant was René, my waiter at the hotel. It was harmless. We were leaving. Who was he going to tell?

When you're exploring, sometimes you'll tell a stranger a secret you're bursting at the seams to share but cannot tell to even your closest friend. The retired dentist you're sitting next to on an airplane. Another couple hiking to the same waterfall. A shoeless tattooist. René.

I've thought a lot about why I love exploring so much. It has little to do with seeing beautiful things and less to do with sitting on airplanes.

What I love about exploration is that it breaks you out of your way of being. A way that you've accepted as your normal, if only by your acquiescence to it. Becoming unknown is a way to test being a different version of yourself.

When was the last time you took an art class, just because? In Toronto, Alison would never give herself permission. Too much to do. Too many people to see. The days pass quickly. But whenever we're in a new place, she explores that side of herself and takes lessons. Mosaic. Silver. Resin. Crochet. Whatever is around.

Everywhere you turn, you are being limited. This can change. You can change your programming. But you can't just know yourself intellectually. You must also know yourself experientially. Shake off the shackles that remind you who you are, or whom you think others think you are, and explore being somebody else for even the shortest bit of time.

An eighty-five-year-old who learned that he was dying once said, "If I had my life to live over again, I'd try to make more mistakes next time. I wouldn't try to be so perfect." Throw out your maps. Don't look it up in advance. Be willing to learn on the fly. You'll make mistakes, scrape your knees, venture in the wrong direction, and be forced to backtrack. Which is a good thing. Burns more calories.

Exploration is not a destination. It's not a checklist of experiences or a collection of passport stamps. It's a way of being—a commitment to remaining perpetually curious, perpetually uncertain, perpetually alive.

We are not meant to be static beings, carefully protecting ourselves from the unknown, sheltered by our own habits and creature comforts. We are meant to be wanderers, investigators, persistent questioners of our own limitations. Every time we choose exploration over comfort, we choose growth. Every time we embrace uncertainty, we evolve.

Your life is not a predetermined path but an ongoing conversation between who you are and who you might become. Exploration is the language of that conversation.

So, go. Get lost. Not just in the world but in yourself. It is essential for your creativity and perspective. Get out there. *There* doesn't require a plane. It's anywhere outside of your routine. The most remarkable journeys have no clear destination—only the promise of discovery.

The reason why I love exploration so much is simple. It's because exploration is the process of being led gently back to myself.

Next, an unbalanced, ambitious, and almost unhinged approach to life-changing transformation.

CHAPTER 1 SUMMARY

- **Escape autopilot through intentional exploration.** True living happens when you break free from a comfortable routine and experience the world (once again) with a childlike wonder.

- **Practice "brailling the world" instead of checking places off a list. Linger, take your time, and immerse yourself fully.** The only way to experience more is by scheduling less.

- **Rank safety third.** Step into uncertainty with intention rather than shrinking from it in fear.

- **Know your instruments and maintain trajectory when lost.** Develop your personal tool kit (language skills, physical preparedness, mental adaptability) and set flexible goals that allow for detours while keeping your general direction.

- **Safely and intentionally introduce uncertainty with the Explorer's Compass.** Start with more tame experiments, progress to moderate challenges, and eventually embrace bold adventures—all while reflecting on how each experience expands your comfort zone.

2.

Define Your Season

Defeat hedonic adaptation through cycles of focus and renewal.

My biggest problem, I've now come to realize, is that it's all so great.

Life. Love. This world. It's amazing.

I want it all.

To build the business, write the book, and grow the muscles. To be an amazing dad, doting husband, and caring grown-up son.

But at the same time, I enjoy aimless walks on the beach, dancing foolishly offbeat, and reading fiction in a comfy chair while sipping overpriced pour-over coffee carefully prepared by a twenty-five-year-old spoken-word poet slash barista.

In Sylvia Plath's *The Bell Jar*, she describes a woman paralyzed beneath a fig tree, starving, unable to choose between the many perfect figs above her, where each fig represents a different future.

One fig is a brilliant career, another is happy marriage, another travel and adventure, and so on. She desperately wants all of them but is paralyzed by indecision. Choosing just one means losing all of the others, she thinks. While she deliberates, the figs wither and fall, opportunities lost to the relentless passage of time.

Life's too short. The moment you focus on one thing, an unshakable guilt for not doing another rears its ugly head.

Unhinged Habits

This chapter offers a radical, almost unhinged, alternative to the myth of balanced improvement: a seasonal approach where focused intensity on one priority replaces scattered consistency across many.

By embracing intense seasons of growth followed by periods of rest or maintenance, you'll make transformative progress in what matters most while keeping guilt at bay. This isn't about doing more—it's about doing less, with greater intensity, at the right time.

The real challenge is never in the gaining. It's in the perception of losing elsewhere else.

Hardworking people often feel stuck because they don't have a definition of what being *unstuck* is. They don't feel joy because they don't know what they're trying to achieve at any given time. They work on a lot, not excited by much. It sucks.

We've been sold on a lie that slow and incremental progress in the pursuit of some faceless better future is the ideal way to make changes.

That we can have it all if we just be more consistent, build better habits, and work a bit harder, day after day, for a long time. It's easy to fill a year this way with chasing down a lot, accomplishing a little.

The longer I live, the more I realize that many more things sound correct than actually are correct. Lots of things make complete sense, and just don't work. Gobstoppers. QR codes as menus. Nickelback's music. I don't accept the power or the impact of marginal, small, daily improvements. It's too nice. Too pretty. Therefore, too unnatural.

Buckle up, because I'm about to challenge a lot of bestselling self-help advice.

Consistency is important, sure. However, I push back on the assertion that it's the most important ingredient in the recipe of success. Lots of people are consistent, yet few get ahead. That's because, borrowing a term from the behavioral change expert Paul Levitan, they're consistently mediocre. "They check the box of 'consistency,' but don't make progress towards their goals because they are consistently coming short of what it takes to move the needle," wrote Levitan.

Getting a bit better every day sounds good. But a more aggressive, intensive, and almost unhinged approach is necessary for transformative change.

Let's start with life's three competing priorities:

1. Money.
2. Health.
3. Relationships.

Consider each priority a side of a triangle. Together, the structure's strong. Ignore one side, and it collapses.

The process of betterment is the process of thickening your triangle, one line at a time, without collapsing the structure.

THE GOLDEN THREE: MONEY, HEALTH, AND RELATIONSHIPS

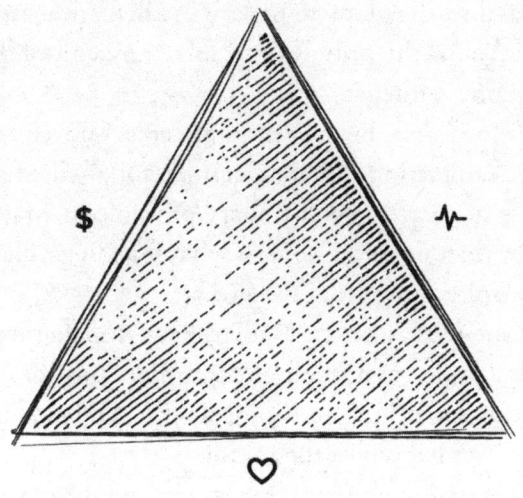

Money, health, and relationships form your life's foundation. Like a triangle, the structure is strong when all three are intact. Remove or ignore one, and the structure collapses. (©Unhinged Habits)

"There is no such thing as work-life balance," wrote the philosopher Alain de Botton. "Everything worth fighting for unbalances your life." Balance, I've come to accept, is for people afraid to burn for something.

Unhinged Habits

Most adults stop evolving once they reach adulthood. They never learn anything new, meaningfully improve their health, or build deep and fulfilling relationships.

Mathematically, the idea of slow gains brought on by stacking habits over time is exponentially positive. And that checks out. The curve is up and to the right, accelerating over time.

Life isn't math. Our brains aren't calculators. Not mine, anyway. Intellectually knowing that something theoretically works is different from living its experience every day.

I'm not able to push a little bit harder every day. I don't even know what that means. On what am I supposed to be improving slowly on? Everything? One thing at a time? And then what, I'm supposed to have blind faith that what I'm doing is going to pay off at some point in the nebulous future, whenever the imaginary curve that governs my life decides to hit an inflection point?

Hope is an opiate, not a plan. That's too much blind faith. Too many unknowns. Even if we are going to make a mathematical argument, I know one thing for certain: the only way to solve any complex problem is to begin with the known integer.

For better or for worse, my human brain craves novelty and excitement and immediate gratification. Maybe I'm not strong-willed enough to overcome thousands of years of evolutionary physiology. Maybe my mind is naturally weaker than others. If so, it is what it is. Regardless, it's up to me to work with the physiology that I've got.

Let's talk about getting better. Like, really getting better. Transforming. Which can only happen as a result of determination—and intensity. Let's talk about wanting something and going after it. Or being okay not having it. Both are fine. Just get out of the middle.

Consistency is undeniably important, but it needs to flank periods of intensity stacked atop one another, focused on one aspect of your life you want to measurably improve.

Seasonality and focus are natural. So is rest.

On/off switches are built into our DNA.

You should have scheduled times for wiping your calendar clean, restarting and reprioritizing. But when you're focused on one thing, you will feel guilty for not doing all the other things, even though you're transforming for the better. It's tough. But I've got a plan for you. And a framework. Lots to cover. Let's dig in.

LIGHTNING STRIKES

I was a personal trainer for eight years. Worked in the fitness industry for nineteen. Saw a lot of people transform their bodies and way more *not* transform their bodies.

Most fail with fitness.

Walk into any gym. Look around. You'll see people working hard, unhappy with their physiques, frustrated that their money and efforts aren't paying off the way they want.

The industry I come from fails most people it tries to serve. It's not for a lack of knowledge or coaches with good intentions. It's because consistency without intermittent bouts of intensity simply doesn't work. It's because we've been sold a lie that physical transformation can be comfortable. That it can be "fit in."

It can't.

Change is hard. If it matters to you, make it matter. If something like transforming your body is important enough to do, at one point, it's gotta be the focus of what you do. Stop squeezing it in like grains of sand around the other big rocks of your life.

In order to start, you've gotta start. That's undeniable. And something is better than nothing. If you're inactive, figuring out any way to move a bit more is going to be a positive. You'll be healthier. Might live longer. Wonderful. Super important.

But if you ask people in the gym why they've shown up that day, many will tell you that their motivation goes beyond improving basic health indicators. They're there because they want to look different. And, sadly, that won't ever happen unless it's a focus.

Transformational change doesn't come about as a result of slow and marginal gains over time. It happens as a result of intensity. Of obsession.

If you put in the dedicated work to build strength and resilience one time, you'll be able to put up with more over time. A transformational period of focus needn't take long to alter a lifetime. Building a strong body requires intense effort. Maintaining a strong body requires consistency.

Ask any super fit person how they got into great shape, and they'll tell you about periods of intensity. A race to prepare for, a photoshoot, or a wedding, perhaps. Then ask this same person if it's relatively easy for them to stay in good shape, and they'll say yes. That's because they've embedded the lifestyle, habits, and newfound self-identity to find comfort and stability in a physiological set point.

I'll say it again: change happens as a result of intensity and is then maintained by consistency.

A rocket burns 90 percent of its fuel during liftoff, fighting Earth's gravity and atmosphere. Once in orbit, it glides effortlessly. New habits follow this cosmic principle: the initial push demands enormous energy to break old routines, but maintain it long enough, and momentum takes over, requiring only minimal adjustments.

Maybe some people are able to do hard things like writing books by fitting it around their other priorities. The math checks out. Five hundred words a day, in theory, takes only thirty minutes. At that rate, a 55,000 word book could be finished in 110 days, or three and a half months. I even mentioned this in my previous book, *The Obvious Choice*.

But there's more to the story.

If my only option were to write a small amount every day, I'd waste time rebooting the book back into my RAM.

By the time I finished trying to remember what I was trying to say, rereading the previous section, and opening up my research and notes, my coffee would be cold, I'd have to pee, and twenty minutes of my thirty-minute writing session would be squandered.

Sure, getting something done is better than nothing. And if that's your only option, then I guess you'll have to figure that out. I hope you do but doubt you will. Which is why even successful people find themselves stuck, never finishing books that they're writing, never transforming their bodies, never learning new skills, and never measurably improving relationships.

I'm in a season of intense effort on this book. If I'm to get it done, it must be a priority. That means waking up early on Sunday morning to write. Because it's a premeditated and defined season, and because it's my choice to do it, I'm excited to drag my body out of bed.

I do try to write every day.

The habit is indeed important to maintain.

Daily reps matter.

If I didn't write something almost daily, my books probably wouldn't get done. But also, my books don't get done *because* I write every day.

The daily efforts—which I call the in-between things—fuel the main thing. But spending all of your time on the in-between things and never focusing on the main thing results in a lot of sticks and no fire. People call this burnout. I've never liked that term. There was never a flame in the first place.

You cannot be passive with that which matters.

If you're trying to meaningfully improve your fitness, the goal of training is to reset your body's "normal" to a higher level of functioning through a relatively short (eight to twelve weeks) dedicated weight training and nutrition program.

If you want to improve a key relationship, let your life be interrupted and go out of your way for that person.

If you want to tackle a big project, commit your best working hours of the week to it. Give yourself full days, uninterrupted, to focus on it each week.

Visually, think of it like this: whenever you're in a season of intensity on one thing, that side is thickening while the other sides are being maintained. And because each season has a priority and focus, it stays fun, fresh, and exciting.

Taylor had been a successful personal trainer for eight years. She loved helping clients transform their bodies but hated the 6:00 a.m.-to-9:00 p.m. schedule that came with it.

At thirty-five, she and her boyfriend were ready for marriage and children. One problem: her income depended entirely on physical presence. No training, no money. The financial reality of family life and personal training didn't compute.

Unhinged Habits

Many tend to think improvement looks like this:

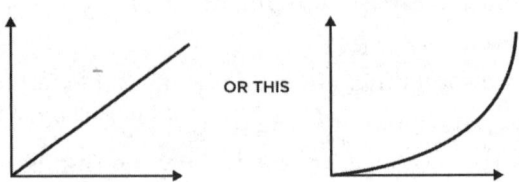

OR THIS

Whereas in reality, it looks more like this:

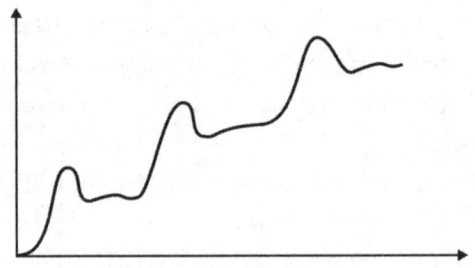

Now, if we were to deconstruct transformation into our three priorities, it more accurately looks like this:

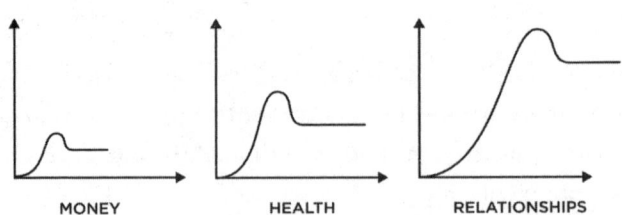

MONEY   HEALTH   RELATIONSHIPS

Pour your energy into growing your money, then shift to physical transformation, then to deepening key relationships, and so on while the other two get placed on steady-state. This intentional seasonal approach allows you to focus, creating real progress without the anxiety that comes with the feeling of what you're neglecting. (©Unhinged Habits)

Define Your Season

Three years earlier, Taylor had bought an online business course from me to escape the time-for-money trap. She dabbled—reading chapters between clients, watching videos before bed—but never gained traction. One online client in three years. Progress measured in molecules.

Then came the wedding date. Suddenly, the future had teeth. With a clear deadline to build a sustainable income before starting a family, Taylor hired my business coaching company and committed to a twelve-week season of intensity.

We didn't teach her anything new. Taylor already knew what to do. What changed was her approach and focus.

Instead of posting generic workout tips that felt like work but led nowhere, she dug deep into identifying exactly who her best clients were. She created detailed profiles of the people who both paid well and were enjoyable to work with.

With this clarity, Taylor made a list of everyone she knew who fit these characteristics. Instead of broadcasting to the void on social media, she reached out individually, asking for advice on the program she was developing. These conversations revealed exactly what her ideal clients actually wanted—information no competitor could access without the same focused effort.

For twelve weeks, she maintained her training schedule but dedicated every evening and weekend to these conversations and building her program. She declined social invitations except for one wedding. She ordered meal delivery to eliminate cooking. Every spare minute went to her business transformation.

The results? After three years of sporadic effort yielding one client, Taylor contracted $21,000 in revenue and fourteen new remote clients in only twelve weeks as a result of her focused intensity.

By her wedding day, she had escaped the time-for-money trap. She'd built an income stream resilient enough to support a growing family.

For Taylor, three years of balance yielded one client. Twelve weeks of intensity created a new life. Her results are common.

With each season your old ceilings will become your new floors, continually circling each element at a higher level. A lightning strike permanently impacting the landscape versus a series of unimpactful sparks.

Unhinged Habits

Whatever it is you want to excel at, whether it's your career, your family, your fitness level, a personal passion, your social life—anything!—define it and prioritize it by placing it at the top of your to-do list.

It's unhinged, almost deranged, this type of maniacal focus.

None of this is likely sustainable long-term both financially or temporally. That's fine. It doesn't need to be.

It's not possible to be in season all the time. You might sometimes have everything on cruise control, too, which is fine.

Long-term consistency and stacking habits is a great way to make sure you do stuff like floss your teeth more often. But without intensity (visits to the dentist), you'll never earn a pearly white smile.

Intensity is for gaining. Consistency is for maintaining. You can't have one without the other.

FEYNMAN'S ANTS

Nature has already solved the problem of how to live seasonally. A solution that the physicist Richard Feynman noticed when he observed ants in his bathroom forming a straight path to their destination.

Feynman then placed a lump of sugar on the opposite side of the tub, far away from the ants' path.

Eventually, an ant found the sugar and returned back to its nest. Feynman tracked its path with a colored marker and saw a wiggly line, full of errors.

Another ant then went for the sugar. Again, Feynman tracked its path back to the nest, this time with a different color marker. It wasn't straight, but had fewer errors than the first.

Feynman repeated this process ten times, noticing that the last few ants formed an efficient and straight line along the rim of the bathtub to the sugar and back to the nest.

"It's something like sketching," he wrote. "You draw a lousy line at first, then you go over it a few times and it makes a nice line after a while."

That's life. That's how you design a good life. You draw a lousy line first. Then you keep going over it until it gets good.

Define Your Season

Success in anything isn't the result of ten thousand hours. It's the result of ten thousand iterations. That's obviously not an exact number. But the idea is correct.

You don't need a perfect plan up front; you sketch. Like a folded piece of paper, the first fold is stiff and awkward, but each subsequent fold over the same crease line becomes easier and faster. Modern life forgives failure. Use that to your advantage.

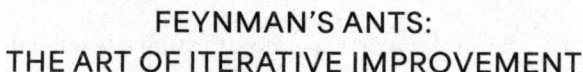

**FEYNMAN'S ANTS:
THE ART OF ITERATIVE IMPROVEMENT**

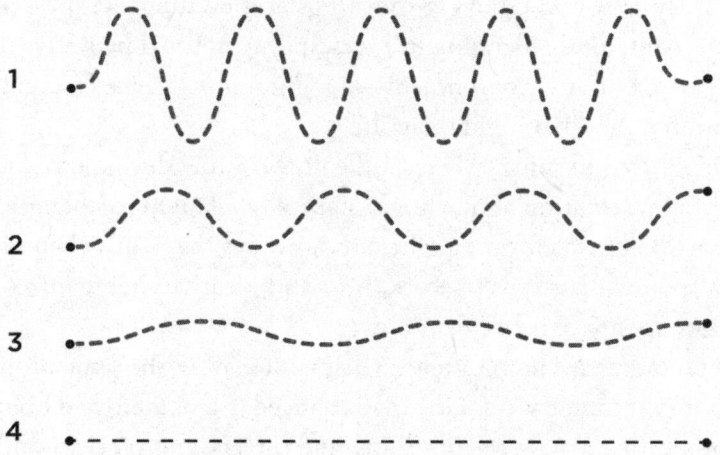

Your habits, relationships, and skills don't develop in straight lines. They emerge through repeated attempts that gradually refine themselves. Start sketching your path now, even if it's imperfect. Excellence comes through iteration. (©Unhinged Habits)

Why we start doing something is never why we continue doing that thing.

We start working out to appease our ego and continue to better our health. With love, like the flickering of a fire, it's the light that first catches our eye, but it's the warmth that keeps us there. And with travel, we start because we want to learn about the world but continue because of what the world teaches us about ourselves.

Unhinged Habits

In my case, travel made me question traditional productivity advice.

Just as those ants found their way around obstacles without a central planner, I discovered that my own productivity and fulfillment didn't require a fixed, unchanging schedule. Instead, it emerged from a responsive relationship with my environment. This revelation challenged everything I thought I knew about consistency and discipline.

My first winter away from Toronto was chaotic. I worked odd hours, overpacked, and overscheduled myself. But with each subsequent season, I refined the process.

In Uruguay, I naturally worked early mornings, leaving afternoons for exploring. In the Dominican Republic, I adapted again—working during the midday heat and enjoying mornings and evenings with loved ones. Without consciously planning it, I was finding optimal pathways through my day based on my environment—a natural intelligence emerging from adaptation rather than rigid structure.

Being forced to constantly reshuffle my priorities during travel revealed something fascinating about how I naturally adapted to changing environments. Like ants forming efficient pathways that shift when obstacles appear, my own patterns of work, rest, and creativity reorganized themselves in response to new constraints.

When I returned home after my first winter away, the same people were worn out in the same ways. Little had changed. All of them had been trying to improve their fitness, relationships, and careers, and yet six months later nothing had changed.

In South India, they used to use hollowed-out coconuts as monkey traps. It'd have a hole just big enough for a monkey's hand and be chained to a stake. The monkey would reach in and grab rice and then couldn't get its hand out. All the monkey needed to do in order to escape was let go of the rice. But it wouldn't let go.

Life wasn't bad for my friends at home, but it wasn't good, either. They were stuck in a trap of comfortable complacency. Bad, but not quite bad enough to force change. Gliding. The most dangerous state of existence.

As much as they tried to keep up, they fell behind. No matter how well they did, it always felt like others were doing better. They were spread too thin, like too little butter over too much bread. Every day for them feeling like a ritual sacrifice to the twin gods of accumulation and accomplishment.

All they had to do was let go and begin sketching a new line. But that's hard to do when your grip inside of the monkey trap is too tight. And so they stayed on the same path, reinforcing the same line—a line that was not fulfilling for them.

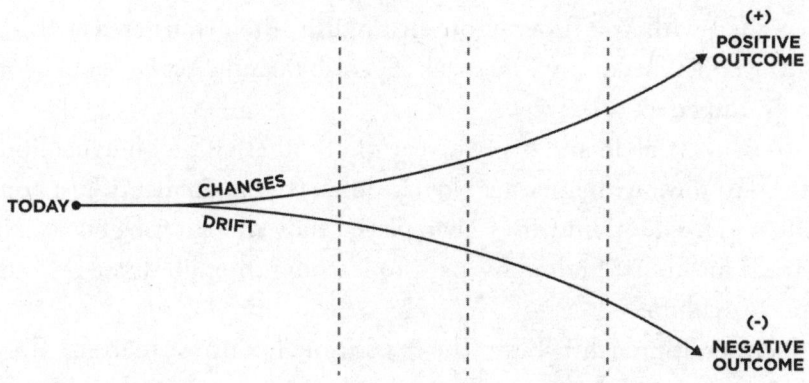

With every day that passes, your grip on your way of being tightens. Each day you delay, your path diverges further. You can always escape and hop the line toward a more positive outcome, but the longer that you wait, the harder it will be as your habits and routines become naturally ingrained over time. (©Unhinged Habits)

Toronto is a hustle culture. People who live here are trying to get ahead. My weeks are full of professional and social responsibilities. It's great. I love it. Until I don't. Then I need to get the heck out.

In the four months when my family lives abroad, we chill. There's no professional or social responsibilities. My calendar is mostly empty.

It's a slower pace.

Unhinged Habits

I read a lot, work out a lot, and walk on the beach a lot. And I actually listen to music. Not as background sound. I sit and I listen. Which I love; until I don't. Then I crave a more frenetic energy, and we get the heck out.

This 8:4 seasonal contrast extends to my son Calvin's education too. During our eight months in Toronto, he attended public school with rigid schedules, structured lessons, and clear rules. Line up. Sit straight. Follow directions.

But during our four-month Mexico season, he attends a jungle school four days a week. In Spanish. A language he barely speaks. He's learning to communicate through body language and raw intention, piecing together meaning without the safety net of fluency.

Last week, he tackled a Charles Darwin assignment in Spanish. He researched with YouTube, wrote in English, then translated word-by-word. Neither he nor my wife speaks Spanish fluently. Yet he read it aloud. Slowly. Imperfectly. Bravely.

Tuesdays, Calvin and his two-year-old brother visit a bilingual library in the next town with my wife. No schedules. No requirements. Just books, crafts, and freedom. Initially, Calvin played endlessly, ignoring books. Now he reads for hours, finding his path to learning through discovery rather than curriculum.

Neither approach is best. The 8:4 seasonal contrast matters. Calvin learns structure and rules in one eight-month season; in the other four months, he forges ahead without guidelines. Children, like adults, need both: times with rigid rules and times of discovery to chart their own course.

What this 8:4 back and forth has taught me is that we can have it all, just not all at once. By dividing the year into distinct eight-month and four-month seasons, we create space for different priorities to take center stage.

Some might wonder: what about the value of consistency? Haven't many achieved greatness through steady, incremental progress rather than seasonal shifts?

I've wondered this myself.

Consistency is undeniably powerful. Essential, even, for maintenance and gradual improvement. The person who meditates for ten minutes a day for years will certainly benefit more than someone who does sporadic three-hour retreats and nothing in between.

But what I've also observed is that true transformation—the kind that reshapes your identity or capabilities—also requires periods of concentrated intensity.

Think of consistency as the reliable foundation that keeps you from sliding backward, while intensity is the force that propels you forward. The writer who writes daily maintains their skill, but the writer who occasionally retreats for weeks of focused creation often produces their breakthrough work during these intensive periods.

"Anxiety isn't the problem, it's the symptom," wrote John Delony in *Building a Non-Anxious Life*. "It's the alarm system letting people know that things are off the rails. If your house is on fire, and the alarm is going off, it's not the alarm that's the problem. It's the house." Before I left Toronto for my first season abroad in 2012, I'd created a world that my brain couldn't exist within. Sure, on the outside I appeared successful. But on the inside, I was spiraling downward: anxious, jealous, and burned-out.

Over the next twelve years, whenever I'd leave Toronto, I packed my backpack, cleared my calendar, and set off. Once it was time to return home, I went through the same process. This duality gave me an opportunity to do a reset—a spring cleaning of sorts—with my calendar and commitments.

The biggest benefit of leaving Toronto each winter and returning home in the spring was the discovery of something I now call 8:4 habits.

Eight months with one focus, four months with another.

The timing can vary; 8:4 isn't about travel. It's about having seasons. Which is about contrast. It's about being excited for the phase you're in, knowing that it's not always the phase you'll be in.

My suggestion to you: Define your season. And the next. Then, dive all-in. You'll be amazed with what you can achieve when you laser in: 5x your focus to 10x your output.

8:4 habits reframe consistency through deliberate seasonal shifts.

What if true consistency isn't about doing the same things every day but rather consistently honoring the natural rhythms of intensity and recovery that our bodies and minds require?

What I propose is that the most sustainable approach is one that plans for both.

And so, at any given time we must be selective of which priority we want to focus on, pursue it aggressively, and be okay with just being okay at anything else . . . for the time being.

There isn't one best way to live. Instead, there are many ways that, counterintuitively, if all we do is that one, lead to burnout.

What I've slowly discovered over the twelve years of my 8:4 seasonal way of living was that I wasn't seeking an escape or chasing year-round sun. I was seeking contrast.

James Danoff-Burg, an entomologist, was asked about Feynman's ant sketching theory. "All things optimize in nature, to some degree," he said. Later, when asked if there was a book to read to learn more about this process, he replied that yes, there is: *On the Origin of Species* by Charles Darwin.

As it turns out, this process of sketching our lives by starting and stopping isn't anything new. It's built into our DNA.

SUNSETS AND BUTLERS

The best sunset that I've ever seen was on the island of Koh Phangan in Thailand.

I first lived there as a poor nomad in 2013. After making good money, Alison and I went back in 2016 and balled out.

We had a butler.

Our home pointed at the setting sun overlooking the Gulf of Thailand. Each night we'd lie on Thai cushions and stare, our sense of self diminished by the wonder of the spectacle in front of us.

Then we stopped noticing the sunset. It was there. I knew it was there. And I'm not sure how long it took for me to stop appreciating it, but it was quick. A week or two. After that, the best sunset that I've ever seen became yet another thing that existed in my world.

Dishwashing machines. Central heating. Fresh orange juice. The platypus. Imagine if you were from another planet with none of those things. Imagine how full of wonder they would all seem. How unjaded you would be by everything amazing in front of you.

Define Your Season

Anhedonia. The inability to feel pleasure. An unfeeling. It comes on passively through hedonic adaptation. Do you know that term? No matter how good or how bad something is, constant exposure to it for even a short period of time causes a numbing. A return to a relatively stable, baseline level of happiness.

Like any evolved system that works for us in some ways, hedonic adaptation works against us in others. It's up to us, therefore, to optimize our lives to work within the constraints of our built-in physiology. Opposing our natural way of being is a ridiculously foolish endeavor.

Every time that I left one place, I found myself excited for the next. If I'd felt burned out in Toronto before I left, I was excited to return—not just excited to sleep in my bed again but excited to reset my schedule, reprioritize my commitments, and start over.

Renewal. The restoring of freshness. When something ends, even for a short period of time, and restarts, you feel invigorated and revitalized. Excited. There's no limit for how often you can repeat this cycle. A new project at work. A weekend away from your family. The beginning of a baseball season (even if your team is perennially disappointing).

Living a seasonal life is nothing new.

Our hunter-gatherer ancestors worked hard in the spring, summer, and fall to collect food and, in the winter, subsisted mostly off their stores. They rested and, I imagine, spent more time with their family and community.

Before Edison invented the light bulb making it possible to be productive past sunset, the average person slept ten hours a night. It varied throughout the year as the seasons changed and the days got longer or shorter. Now the average person gets six to seven hours of sleep *year-round*.

The invention of the lightbulb, combined with the clock, caused natural time to take a back seat to artificial time.

Every day became the same: nine to five. Clock in, clock out, ignoring the seasonal rhythms of our bodies. Numbing and scrolling to the point where we feel like a zombie instead of replenishing ourselves in healthy ways. In a search for efficiency, we've become more machine, less human. It's mechanistic. Unnatural.

Unhinged Habits

No wonder we burn out.

Goethe once said, "Wherever a man may happen to turn, whatever a man may undertake, he will always end up by returning to that path which nature has marked out for him." We're wired for the world we evolved in. How the world was. Not how the world is.

We're wired to have seasons.

Stops.

Starts.

Periods of work followed by periods of rest.

Without contrast, we are blind. Silence is part of the music. The dark is how we see the light.

Spend part of your day going fast. Crush a workout. Dive deep into your work. Spend the rest of your day going slow. Walk. Read. Get coffee with a friend. Avoid the anxious middle, never fully on, never fully off. This is the essence of 8:4 habits.

It's natural to work hard and go all-in on one thing, obsess over it, and get tired. Tired is good. But then you need to rest, recover, and sketch a different line, renewing your energy like a sprouting spring flower in early May.

Burnout exists because the clock created artificial time and removed the seasonality we've been hardwired to crave. This, combined with too much stimulus of the same kinds—the same routine, work, people, and pleasures—extended over long enough periods of time leads to a lack of appreciation for even the greatest things.

Nature abhors a vacuum. If there's an empty space, physically, metaphorically, or temporally, we fill it. Addition is natural; subtraction is not. Over time, responsibilities add up, commitments compound, and the stuff we own tends to own us.

I said earlier that we start traveling to learn about the world but continue because of what the world teaches us about ourselves. What the world taught me was that, when you start and stop (in my case, literally packing up and leaving), it's a forced moment to reassess your priorities. Ejecting you out of your autopilot so that you can lock in on your obsession for this season.

Define Your Season

If you want to go to bed tired, not exhausted, ready for sleep but excited to get back up and do it all again, the question you must ask yourself is not whether you should have seasons but how.

AN OFF-SEASON CHECKLIST

If you want to transform your fitness in the next twelve weeks, hire a trainer, measure your food, and exercise four to six times a week while getting to bed by 10:00 p.m. each night and abstaining from alcohol.

Your social life would be affected. And your work. And your wallet. It's not a sustainable plan.

But you'll be focused. It'll be fun because you'll see and feel changes to your body. And after twelve weeks, you'll be transformed. You'll feel great. Like a new person. Evolved. Stack a few of these seasons on top of one another over time (a break in between is fine), and you'll be amazed at what you've accomplished in a relatively short period of time.

I'm in a season of writing. It's three months long. I hope to mostly finish the first draft of this book.

Four mornings a week, I wake up early to write for two hours. Before bed, I review my notes and plan the next day's writing. Three days a week (Mondays, Thursdays, and Fridays) my entire work day is dedicated to this book. I have no meetings, no phone calls, and I don't respond to emails.

It's aggressive. There's a lot I miss out on when I'm in season. But this book is important to me. It's hard. Anything worth doing is hard. I'm creatively challenged. Which means that I'm creatively fulfilled. When I'm in season on a book, I can't wait to get out of bed. When you're in season on anything, you can't wait to get out of bed.

But you also can't ignore the other areas of your life.

The other two sides of the triangle (relationships and fitness) can't be ignored during a season of focus on money. They just get put into off-season mode. Call it consistency. There's also things that I need to do for work other than this book.

Whenever you enter an 8:4 season, also create an off-season checklist. Things that need to get done in order for you to feel comfortable

Unhinged Habits

committing obsessively on your priority. It keeps my fear-based brain at bay, knowing that what has to get done is getting done.

Here's my off-season checklist while I'm in season on this book:

Relationships
- Daily breakfast and dinner with family
- Daily one-on-one play with each kid for fifteen minutes (minimum)
- Weekly date night with Alison
- Weekly text or call to a friend to say hello
- Weekly dinner with friends or neighbors
- Three weekly "out-of-the-blue" compliments to colleagues or team members

Fitness
- Three weekly full-body workouts
- No more than two coffees a day
- Weekly zone 2 cardio session (long bike ride or jog)

Money
- Publish my free *5-Reps Friday* newsletter weekly
- Record *The Obvious Choice* podcast
- Publish to Instagram four times a week
- Prepare for, and attend, all team meetings
- Approve payroll

At the end of last week, I glanced at my list and noticed that I hadn't sent the compliments. That forced me to think of three people. Which I did. And I sent them a nice message. Took five minutes.

Of course, you'll miss the mark sometimes. When you get offtrack; when your brain jumps into fear mode; when the walls feel like they're closing in—that you're missing out, screwing up, not doing what you have to do, look at your checklist, take a deep breath, and get back on track.

Another example. This time of a short season.

My brother and I grew up together. He's eighteen months older. We shared a bedroom until we were fourteen. Then he went to Nova Scotia and met a girl. They got married. He stayed.

We message a bit. Not enough. I'm not good at staying in touch with faraway family. That's not a nice thing to admit.

I used to beat myself up about being bad at staying in touch. But then I realized that it is what it is, and as much as I don't like this part of me, it's not a part that's going to change. Instead of trying to slowly improve my relationship with my brother over time, we took a trip to Halifax.

One week, full immersion. My family and his.

I didn't work out, just went for walks. I read a lot but didn't write. All work meetings were canceled. The only "work" I did was reposting old content to Instagram a few times.

Seasons don't have to be long, but they have to be intense. I feel close to my brother again. Like I have a brother again.

You may be thinking that this is impossible with your current demands and commitments. Parents of young children. A busy job. Financial constraints. Or some other reason. And it's possible that you're right. Perhaps now isn't the time.

But when resources are limited—whether time, money, or energy—focused intensity becomes a necessity, not a luxury. The harder your circumstances, the more essential it becomes to stop spreading yourself thin.

Will it be easy? No. Nothing worthwhile ever is. But consider the alternative: continuing to make minimal progress across multiple fronts, year after year, never getting ahead.

The 8:4 principles of seasonality and focused intensity can be adapted to any life circumstance. Here are some practical applications:

For Parents with Young Children

Try taking a Microseasons Approach: Instead of 8:4 months, test out 6:2 week cycles or maybe even 30:10 day sprints. For example, try dedicating thirty days to intensely focus on a career project while maintaining baseline parenting duties, then shift focus to family enrichment for the next ten days with special outings or quality time.

Synchronize Your Seasons with Your Partner: Coordinate complementary seasons, where one takes on more household/childcare responsibilities while the other intensifies focus on personal development or career advancement. This creates a fair rhythm where both partners get opportunities for focused growth. Just make sure that you also do a season focused on one another.

Seasonal Childcare Investments: For a defined eight-to-twelve-week season, invest in additional childcare. The temporary nature makes the expense more manageable, and the clear time boundary helps manage guilt. Three months of additional childcare might yield years of benefits from your focused progress.

For Those with Demanding Careers

Project-Based Seasons: Corporate professionals can align seasonal focus with natural business cycles. Schedule an intensive relationship or health season during quieter business periods, for example.

Weekend Intensity: Dedicate entire weekends to seasonal focus on a side hustle or a relationship in a concentrated time frame, while maintaining career demands during weekdays.

Vacation Season Intensives: Instead of taking a day off here and a day off there, batch your time off and take longer breaks for one to two weeks of complete immersion. Use accumulated time off for transformation rather than relaxation—a fitness camp, writing retreat, or relationship reconnection—creating compressed seasons of growth.

For Those with Financial Constraints

Investment Seasons Versus Harvest Seasons: Alternate between seasons that require financial investment (education, equipment, coaching) and seasons focused on monetizing those investments. This creates a sustainable cycle where each investment season is funded by the previous harvest season.

Community-Based Seasons: Partner with others in similar situations to share resources during intensive seasons—childcare swaps, skill exchanges, or accountability groups that multiply individual capacity without additional cost.

Bartering Seasons: Dedicate a season to leveraging what you already have to get what you need. Trade your existing skills, time, or assets for the resources necessary for your transformation. For example, offer social media management to a fitness coach in exchange for training.

The specifics don't matter as much as the commitment to focused seasons. Whatever your circumstances, find the approach that works for you. The alternative—remaining perpetually scattered across all priorities—guarantees stagnation.

Like Feynman's ants, you must sketch. Each season, thicken a side of your triangle while all else goes on cruise control, not ignored, but not being aggressively pursued.

This unbalanced, ambitious, and almost unhinged approach, counterintuitively, leads to a more balanced life.

THE PERFECT CALENDAR

Over the course of a season, you'll add obligations, tasks, and responsibilities. Stuff. Just stuff. You'll buy stuff. Accumulate stuff. Commit to stuff. But rarely, if ever, will you subtract stuff. If you're in a never-ending season, odds are, you'll be never-ending adding.

End your seasons. Each end, a new beginning.

Design time to review, reassess, reprioritize, and remove in order to reenergize.

For twelve years, at least twice a year, as I came and went from Toronto, I wiped my calendar clean and started new.

Do I still need to own this? Is that weekly meeting impactful? Am I happy with the time I'm spending with my kids? Every move forced me to pause, hit the reset button, and reevaluate my priorities not as they were, but as they are.

Unhinged Habits

The software company Asana once had a "meeting doomsday." They asked all employees to delete every meeting, sit with their empty calendar for forty-eight hours, and repopulate their calendars only with meetings they deem valuable.

Which is great. Because meetings suck.

"We found that when employees were given the freedom to step back and assess, they changed many of their meetings to be shorter, unconventional lengths (like fifteen minutes). They also changed the cadence of meetings to be less frequent," wrote Rebecca Hinds, the head of Asana's Work Innovation Lab.

Asana reported that employees saved, on average, eleven hours a month, or seventeen workdays a year, the equivalent to a three-and-a-half week vacation.

Most of what we do we don't really need to be doing; we've just been doing it for so long that it's become a thing that we do, and we don't ever think about whether it needs to actually be done.

Evaluate what's on your calendar. Has it been properly designed? Or is it the result of a smattering of stuff you've committed to over the years? Each week, are you going through the motions for reasons you've long since forgotten? If so, perhaps it's time to end your cycle of passivity and make some hard decisions.

I stumbled upon this spring cleaning system by accident. Over the years, I began to recognize its value and refined my system.

Now that we've explored how 8:4 habits can transform your relationship with consistency, intensity, and personal growth, let's pause to apply these insights to your own life. The following worksheet will help you identify which areas of your life might benefit from this seasonal rhythm and help you begin sketching your own path.

Define Your Season

SEASON STARTER WORKSHEET

1. **Define your season**

   Season Length: _____ weeks/months of focus, followed by _____ weeks/months of reset

   Priority: (Circle one) MONEY | HEALTH | RELATIONSHIPS

   My Focus: _____

2. **Create your plan**

   Best Hours: I will dedicate _____ (am/pm) to _____ (am/pm) on these days: _____

   Transformation Activity:

   _____
   _____

   Resources Needed: (What support, tools, or expertise do you need?)

   _____
   _____

3. **Build your off-season checklist**

   Health Maintenance: (Minimum activities to stay healthy)

   _____
   _____

   Relationship Maintenance: (Minimum activities to maintain connections)

   _____
   _____

   Money/Work Maintenance: (Minimum activities to maintain stability)

   _____
   _____

Unhinged Habits

4. Manage fear of missing out and guilt

    My "Later List": (Ideas or opportunities you want to do and will revisit for future seasons)

    _____

    _____

To download an expanded version of the Season Starter worksheet, go to www.Jonathangoodman.com/season.

Once you enter into a season, wipe your calendar clean and start over as if it's day one. Imagine you don't have any commitments and that this is the first time that you've scheduled anything in.

Here's the order I recommend for rebuilding your calendar:

1. Fitness comes first
2. Have to do
3. In-season priority
4. Need to do
5. Outsource / delegate / hire out / ignore

A bit more on each.

Define Your Season

1. Fitness comes first

Figure out where, how, and when you're going to exercise for the coming season. Once that's in, everything else (when to eat, work schedule, childcare, and so on) tends to naturally fall into place.

Fitness might not be the most important thing in your life. But the easiest way to build your calendar from the ground up is to schedule it first.

2. Have to do

My parents have been married for more than fifty years.

I'm the youngest of four. The house was hectic. Dad traveled a lot for work. We kids had different extracurriculars. Grandparents passed. Life happened.

Despite the insanity, by all accounts, Mom and Dad are still in love today.

"In those crazy busy years, how did you make time for one another?" I asked Mom.

"We went for morning walks," she said.

She told me that once my sister got old enough to be home alone, she and Dad woke up early and went for a walk together, just the two of them.

"That was our only time to connect for years," Mom said.

Groceries, house cleaning, childcare, laundry—all while trying to be the best spouse, sibling, parent, grown-up child . . . there's a lot to deal with.

After fitness, plug in the thing(s) you have to do. I don't need to tell you what they are. You already know.

3. In-season priority

If you're in an 8:4 season, commit your best work hours to your most important priority. This could be an aspect of your day job but isn't necessarily one.

4. Need to do

What you'll be left with is everything you think that you need to do. Things like preparing for meetings, administration, email, and, of course, personal responsibilities.

Generally, these are low-cognition tasks that can be relegated to the time of the day when your brain no work so good no more.

An example.

I'm useless after 11 a.m. If you get an email response from me, it's probably going to be after that.

5. Outsource, delegate, hire out, ignore

Finally, you'll be left with things you think need to get done that you don't want to do. They either aren't important, or they require a brain that works differently than yours.

Some of the tasks could probably be ignored. Replace the others by delegating, automating, or hiring out. As Dan Martell says, "Eighty percent done by someone else is 100 percent awesome."

Every time I clear my calendar I put less back in it. After twelve years, the result's a mostly empty schedule with three days a week completely clear. This works for me. Your perfect calendar will look different from mine. The only way for you to figure it out is to reliably clear it at least twice a year and repopulate it back from nothing.

Each time you leave one season and enter another, repeat the process starting with an evaluation of how the last period went. Nothing fancy: phone off; pen and paper; three questions.

1. What felt good?
2. Where did I feel resistance?
3. What can I eliminate next season?

Every iteration gets you closer to your perfect. With each season, you'll become more aligned with how you work best, more focused on your priority, and more energized because you'll be doing more of what fuels you and less of the accumulated crap that inevitably builds up over time.

It's something like sketching.

COFFEE GROUNDS AND EXPENSIVE FRAGRANCES

Whenever I was being a good dad, son, husband, or friend, I'd get this unshakable feeling of guilt for not showing up in my business as much as I'd like to.

Other times, if I was committing myself to my business, I'd feel guilt for not giving that same attention to my family.

And in both cases, my fitness would suffer.

Then I'd put effort into my fitness and feel guilty for not putting that same effort into work and family.

Brains. Man! Always guilt-tripping me like a Jewish grandma over a missed Shabbat call.

Most often, what we desire in life devolves into obligations: I have to succeed at work or else I'll fail myself or my family; I have to exercise or else I won't be attractive; I have to make time for my loved ones or else I'm not a good person.

Focus is a superpower. We all know this intuitively. But, weirdly, focus comes with guilt.

You'll always have more information on the area you're focusing on than the ones you're not. This comparative ignorance—this asymmetry of knowledge for *the other thing* you're not doing—creates the illusion that the grass is greener.

It wasn't always this way.

Our screens have shattered life's natural boundaries. Your boss's urgent email, your mother's health update, and your fitness app's guilt trip all scream for attention from the same pocket. Right now. Every day. All day. This digital assault extracts a brutal psychological toll: be everywhere, optimize everything, never rest.

The "just be consistent" mantra was born in a quieter era. It never accounted for attention as today's most precious currency or how ruthlessly it's being hijacked. We're using factory-floor productivity rules in a notification-tsunami reality. It doesn't account for how our attention has been weaponized against us, fractured into a thousand notifications, each promising that this email, this post, this message is the one that demands immediate attention.

Unhinged Habits

"The rate of technological change is now accelerating so fast that it has risen above the average rate at which most people can absorb these changes," wrote Astro Teller, the "Head of Moonshots" at Google X, a semisecret research and development facility aiming to make the world a radically better place.

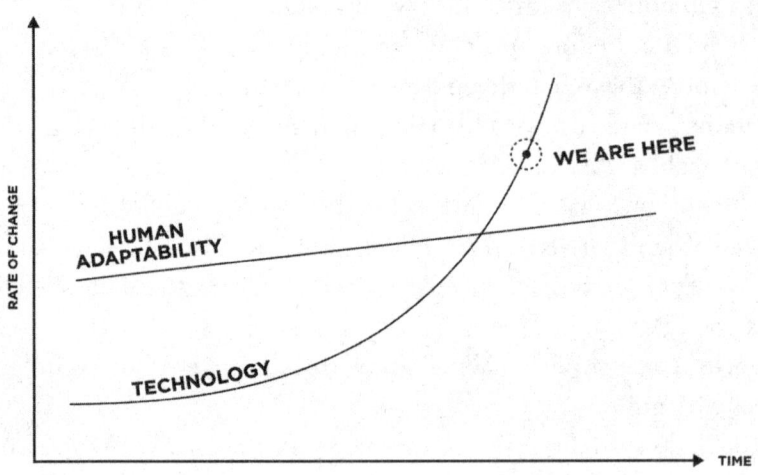

Technological evolution is outpacing human adaptability. When the rate of change is too quick to process, angst results. (Adapted from *Thank You for Being Late* by Thomas Friedman)

It's an impossible-to-win race, one not worth taking part in. I don't know where you are right now. I don't know anything about you. We're in a different year, you and I. Despite all of this, I know that there's a lot you feel like you're missing out on right now. And I know that you're anxious about it.

Regressing to a state of blindness by pathologically narrowing your exposure obviously isn't the answer, nor is it possible. Feeling like you're missing out is unavoidable. And, though it doesn't necessarily feel like it, it's a good thing.

"There is consolation in the fact that missing out is an inexorable side effect of the richness of human life," wrote Kieran Setiya in *Midlife*. "It reflects something wonderful: that there is so much to love and that it is so various that one history could not encompass it all."

Okay, cool. I like philosophy. It helps me make sense of the problem when I've drunk enough coffee to read dense enough books that make sense of the problem. But it still doesn't tell me what I can do.

The answer is 8:4 habits. Dynamic stability. Contrast. Stopping and starting. Seasons. No matter how great something is or tastes or smells or feels, we need palate cleansers. Coffee grounds between sampling expensive fragrances.

It's not perfect. Fear of missing out is unavoidable. The grass will always be greener. But so long as you actively seek contrast—the difference between two things—you'll be more excited for what you're currently doing and less fearful of what you're not because you know that its time will come.

MORE OF LESS

I wrote fifteen million words on the internet from 2011 to 2024. During that period, 90 percent of my income came from one program and most of my reputation from one book.

But if I just created that program and just wrote that book, much of the good that ended up coming from them wouldn't have happened.

The part that's missing from the famous Pareto Principle—the 80/20 rule where 80 percent of your success comes from 20 percent of your actions—is that you still have to do the 80 in order to figure out what the 20 is. Then, once you figure it out, go all in. Outsized efforts flanked by years of consistently good enough actions are the key.

Intensity grows; consistency maintains.

If I were to ask you whether you'd prefer $50 or $100, you'd choose $100. The two outcomes are similar enough to be compared. One of them is obviously better than the other.

Most decisions that we make with what to do with our time aren't like that though. They're harder to make sense of because they cannot be compared. Therefore, they come with an uncompensated loss.

Unhinged Habits

If I wake up early to work on this book, I might not recover from my workout as well from the day before. What impact will that have on how I feel, my long-term health, or my short-term levels of sexification on a completely subjective scale of how I feel I look from 1–10? I've no idea. The loss, therefore, is uncompensated. Incomprehensible. Impossible to calculate.

An 8:4 habits approach isn't about perfection—it's about permission.

Permission to be gloriously unbalanced in pursuit of what matters most.

Permission to let some areas coast while others transform.

Permission to sketch your life with bold, imperfect strokes rather than tentative, careful ones.

Our world pulls us in countless directions, demanding perpetual progress across every domain. But true transformation rebels against this pressure. In an age where we are overwhelmed by what the psychologist Barry Schwartz refers to as the "paradox of choice," it comes as an enormous relief to proactively designate a period of time focused on leveling up some aspect of the money, health, or relationships side of our triangle, knowing that another time will come for our other priorities.

It's this reduction in guilt that makes your life finally feel freeing. Within each season, you grant yourself permission to do more of less. Which, over time, is the only way to have more.

Next, how a thirty-two-year-old small-business owner and father of five reads a novel a week.

CHAPTER 2 SUMMARY

- **Prioritize focused intensity over scattered consistency.** True transformation comes from periods of intense, almost unhinged focus on a single priority rather than marginal improvements across many fronts.

- **Work with your natural rhythms, not against them.** Humans are wired for seasonality—periods of intensity followed by recovery and renewal. Respecting these cycles leads to greater fulfillment and prevents burnout.

- **Strengthen one life priority at a time.** Focus intensely on improving one area (money, health, or relationships) while maintaining a baseline in the others. Over time, each dimension of your life strengthens through dedicated seasons.

- **Schedule regular calendar resets.** Twice a year, wipe your calendar clean and rebuild it intentionally. Reprioritize your time based on your current season's focus, removing previous commitments that no longer serve you.

3.

Make More Mistakes

*Embrace the humility of
the unknown.*

The more we know, the less we tend to admit we don't know.

The older we get, the less we tend to explore, learn, and experience. And the smaller our world tends to become.

That's because, the older we get, the more pressure we tend to feel to optimize the life we're living for productivity, efficiency, and certainty.

But what if the path to more meaning isn't found through ever-increasing productivity but through periods of strategic (un)productivity?

What you're about to read is an invitation for you to create space. To pause and to check out. Because checking out tends to be the best way to check in.

First, a question:

What year was Ghandi born?

If you don't know the answer, that's fine. It's not Tuesday night trivia at Trixie's Cantina. Instead, what's the earliest year you think he could have been born? And then the latest year you think he could have been born. The range.

Unhinged Habits

When Jason Feifer, the editor in chief of *Entrepreneur Magazine*, was asked this question, he said 1940–1955. He was wrong.

Knowing when Ghandi was born isn't important. "What's important is to know how confident you should be in the knowledge you think you have," said Warren Hatch, the CEO of a forecasting company called Good Judgment.

Let's build on this question.

How confident are you in the knowledge that drives your life's direction?

How confident are you in what you believe to be true?

How confident are you that the people you surround yourself with are the right people for you to be surrounding yourself with?

How confident are you that you've explored enough of other people's worlds to know how to best exist in your own?

Feifer asks the Ghandi question both in talks to executives at Fortune 500 companies and on college campuses. According to him, there's a fascinating difference in how it's answered between audience groups.

When he's talking to experienced professionals, their answers all have tight bands, fifteen-to-twenty-year ranges. But then he does this with college students . . . And they'll say, "Uh, I don't know. 1800–1900." They'll throw out hundred-year, two-hundred-year, or even five-hundred-year ranges.

Everybody starts laughing. But did you catch the most important part of what they said?

Three words: "I don't know."

The more you know, and the more you've achieved, the more you'll feel pulled to move throughout the world with the self-directed expectation that you *should* have the answer. When it comes to Ghandi's birth year, there's a right answer and a wrong one. With life, there isn't. The best you can do is make a best guess. And so, you must program yourself to go into any situation where, even if you don't know everything—and you never will—you won't have an unhealthy level of false confidence.

Said another way: admit your ignorance.

Young people tend to be better than older people at this. They have no expectation that they know the answer, and therefore it's perfectly reasonable for them to just have wild guesses. And those wild guesses are basically them saying, "I don't know." "I have no idea."

They explore more, take more risks, and make more mistakes.

Incredibly, the result of all of this is that they also stumble upon brilliance more.

None of us have basically any idea about anything. That's because it's impossible to basically have any idea about anything. When faced with something we don't understand, which is basically everything, the most natural thing to do is to be afraid and pretend stuff makes sense when it doesn't. The correct way to exist, and the more interesting way to exist, is to admit you have no clue what's going on and then go with it.

This is the essence of religion. It's the delegation of understanding. We call it belief—belief in a higher power to help deal with an impossibly complicated and mysterious existence.

An example of something that we use every day that nobody really understands:

The lightbulb was invented only 145 years ago. One hundred forty-five years ago, nighttime was dark. Like, the sun set, and you went to bed because you couldn't see.

How often do you stub your toe these days because it's dark? Not often, right? People back then must've stubbed their toes *all the time*. Then some guy came along and was like, "I can make a fire inside of a glass tube that melts a wire but doesn't melt the wire too quickly, and when that happens it'll create light at night so you don't stub your toe anymore."

One more example:

Your phone is a box made out of materials dug out of the ground. When you tap on it, it sends a signal to space. Space then says what's up and responds with any piece of entertainment or information known to humankind.

Everybody, everywhere, every time that they use their phone should just be screaming, *"How is this happening?"* as they watch videos of seventeen-year-olds from Korea beatboxing.

Your phone is magic. It's literally magic. We can harness it and re-create it. We use it. But nobody really understands it.

Most everything is like that, when you think about it.

Unhinged Habits

I've got this friend who visited me in Kotor, Montenegro, when my family lived there. I'll call him Dak Mitchum because I've always wished that I knew somebody with a name like Dak Mitchum.

We walked through the gates into old town, and Dak and his girl went straight to a Turkish store selling fake purses. They were there for three hours, debating endlessly about the stitching and zippers and whether it'd pass for the real thing.

Later that day, I posted a pic of us together and got this message:

Is your boy Dak Mitchum a good person? His relationship with money and the need to discuss it publicly isn't exactly in line with the person you typically surround yourself with. Always been fascinated by the guy but have a hard time imagining I could enjoy his company.

"Bro," I typed back. "I just spent *three hours* with him and his girl in a Turkish store in Montenegro that sells fake purses and at the end, they didn't buy a thing. And you know what? I couldn't look away. I was enthralled. They were so into it. Dak's unabashedly himself. And he doesn't give a shit who notices. I really enjoy people like that."

"So here's a really stupid thing about the world," wrote Hank Green in *A Beautifully Foolish Endeavor*. "The trick to looking cool is not caring whether you look cool. So the moment you achieve perfect coolness is simultaneously the moment that you actually, completely don't care."

What I realized that day in Montenegro wasn't Dak's shopping habits. It was about how refreshing it is to be around somebody who lives entirely in their own world, following their own rules.

At first, I was impatient in that purse store. Then I found myself admiring how Dak and his girlfriend were fully present in their experience. In that moment, Dak taught me something vital about checking in by checking out: he wasn't performing for anyone.

Dak Mitchum doesn't care what you think about him.

Dak Mitchum will be in Kotor only for two days and yet spends his first three hours there debating with a Turkish merchant over how real his fake purses look before deciding that the stitching isn't close enough to the real thing and walking out.

Then Dak Mitchum will say that he's hungry, and you'll go to a restaurant with him, and he'll order cheese pasta and ask for extra cheese, and when it comes, he'll tell the waiter that it still isn't cheesy enough and ask for more cheese on the side.

He wasn't rushing to the next tourist spot or worried about optimizing his vacation. Instead, the guy was completely immersed in exactly what interested him, social expectations be damned.

Being stuck . . . It's an artificial constraint; an imaginary island floating in a fluid world—the most hopeless prison. Being stuck isn't a place you're forced into by someone else but a jail into which you enter voluntarily, lock the door, and throw away the key. A prison where the older you get, the less you tend to explore, and the tighter the lock gets.

There's no steady state. You're expanding or constricting; loosening or tightening. When we overestimate our knowledge, we make decisions based on fantasy, not reality.

When we say, "I know this," the next thing that happens seems benign: "Because I know this, I'm going to do that." And then it keeps going. "Because I'm doing that, I'm surrounded by these people." Followed by, "Because I'm surrounded by these people, I also know this." The consequences compound.

Before long, you're lost on your island, surrounded by people who think like you and act like you, self-assured in your mutual delusion.

Meanwhile, the rowboat you desperately need to escape has been there the entire time, just out of sight, hidden behind some bushes you never thought to look behind.

College students tend to be less afraid to admit their ignorance. Sometimes this gets them into trouble, but even if it does, it's never that serious over the long term.

Have you ever heard of Murphy's Law? Everything that can go wrong will go wrong. I haven't found that to be true. Instead, I've found its inversion more accurate. Call it Yhprum's Law: Everything that can work out will work out.

Unhinged Habits

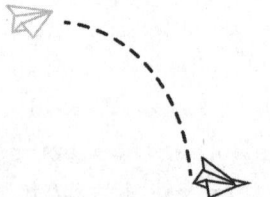

MURPHY'S LAW

Everything That Can Go Wrong Will Go Wrong.

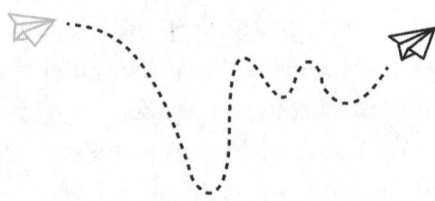

YHPRUM'S LAW

Everything That Can Work Out Will Work Out.

> *While Murphy's Law makes us fear the worst, Yhprum's reminds us that life has a funny way of working out for people willing to try things, often in ways we couldn't have planned. That even when our plans fall apart, it often results in something wonderful.* (©Unhinged Habits)

Young people explore more, take risks more, and do stupid things more because they're less afraid to admit when they don't know something. Incredibly, the result of all of this is that they also have more fulfilling and varied experiences. Perhaps that's one reason why many refer to their earlier years as the best time of their life.

The Ghandi problem demonstrates a rising overconfidence as we age. The more you learn, and the more success that you achieve, the more narcissistically protective of your way of being that you'll become.

You would have gotten the Ghandi question right if you admitted that you had no idea. Because then you could have answered confidently with a wider band. Once admitting your ignorance, you could have said, "I've no idea. Uh, sometime between the year 1600 and the year 2000." That would have been *correct*. Ghandi was born in 1869. A four-hundred-year range would have been the *correct answer*.

SEEKING SERENDIPITY

There's a passage written in the *Journal of Humanistic Psychology* by an eighty-five-year-old man who learned that he was dying that I can't get out of my head: "If I had my life to live over again, I'd try to make more mistakes next time. . . . I'd start barefoot earlier in the spring and stay that way later in the fall."

We revel in denying ourselves. "If it's not a hell yes, it's a no," many advise, missing the necessary nuance.

Productivity isn't the struggle. Having something worth being productive for is. Admittedly, saying yes to more isn't productive. It does, however, lead to more serendipity.

Fine, I say. Less productivity, more serendipity.

Meander more. Walk barefoot in the grass more. Stop and watch the sunset more. And if somebody else is getting ahead because they've decided to work nights and weekends and you didn't, smile and say "good for you" more.

There's this old saying that goes "the unlived life is not worth living." Well, an overly productive life is not worth living, either. But the unbalanced life . . . the 8:4 life . . . is absolutely worth living. Because the unbalanced life is full of meaningful work, serendipity, exploration, and wonder.

When you rely on yourself to make decisions based on the *hell yes, or no* heuristic, you're resting on your biases and creature comforts.

"Hell yes" is always going to be your response if it's something within your familiar confines. "No" is always going to be your response if it's something different, unfamiliar, and therefore scary.

When you say yes, you won't like everything that you do.

Last night, my wife and I ended up in the Ethiopian part of town. We shared a dish at a traditional restaurant. The food wasn't good. I got fried chicken after.

Some stuff will be a drag, some hard, and sometimes you'll wish you went for tacos. But it'll expose you to more things, people, and opportunities. And who knows, maybe you'll like some of it. Like pickleball; what a silly little fun game. Or Spanish guitar. Or jogging.

Unhinged Habits

People always quote Warren Buffet to me whenever I talk about this. He said that "the difference between successful people and really successful people is that really successful people say no to almost everything."

And maybe it's true. I'd have to know how he defined *really successful* though. Having read multiple biographies of the man, I find his definition of success very different from mine. Which is fine.

Even without debating the merits of financial or professional success versus personal, most people aren't anywhere close to the professional level where they should be saying no to most of what comes their way. But what if you are? And how would you even know?

John Berardi bootstrapped a company from nothing and sold it for close to $200 million. Then he retired to become a full-time dad, youth athletic coach, and carpool driver.

According to Berardi, there are five stages of yes:

Stage one: When rare opportunities come along, everything is a yes. You don't have the luxury of saying yes or no because no one's offering you anything. You need the reps in order to figure out what you like doing. You need to discover what you find rewarding versus what you *think* you'll find rewarding.

Stage two: Opportunities are starting to come to you. Now, unless it's a *hell no*, everything is a yes. As long as the person doesn't suck, it's not illegal, or it couldn't hurt your reputation, go for it.

Stage three: Opportunities are coming faster now. Choose the ones that pay off financially or emotionally.

Stage four: Too many opportunities. Focus on your ambitious goals and value system. Be kind, but ruthlessly turn down almost everything.

Stage five: Overwhelmed with requests. You're beyond saying no. Other people must do it on your behalf. Build a rubric and have people evaluate opportunities on your behalf.

THE FIVE STAGES OF "YES"

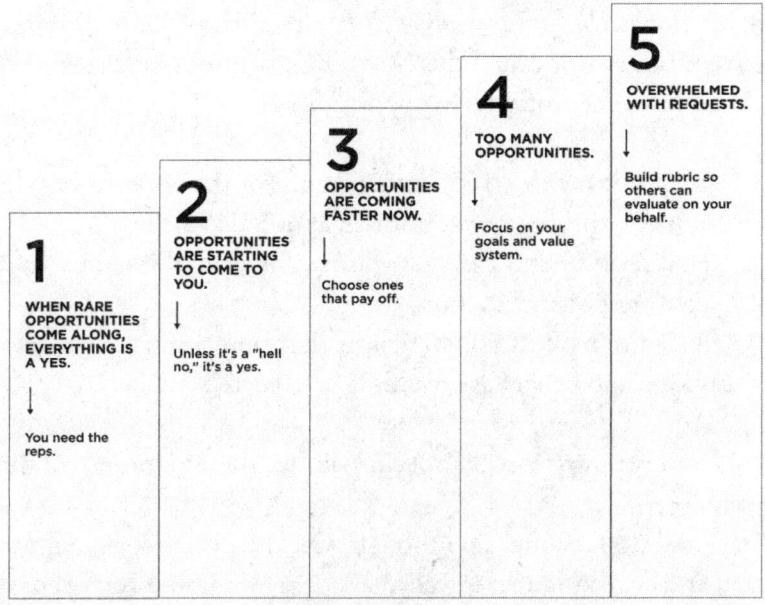

Your relationship with professional opportunities naturally transforms as you progress in your career. Understanding your current stage helps you make appropriate decisions without guilt and prepare for what comes next. (©Unhinged Habits)

Also worth noting, when starting a new gig you tend to start over at stage one, regardless of previous success or notoriety.

Reputation is highly contextual. What we perceive as "global status" is actually a collection of microreputations, each confined to its own ecosystem.

Your authority isn't a portable asset you carry from space to space—it's deeply embedded in the relationships, history, and social proof you've built within specific communities.

This isn't just about fame or follower counts; it's true for all forms of credibility: The respected professor who switches universities and has to reestablish classroom rapport. The business leader who moves industries and finds their expertise questioned. The community leader who moves homes and becomes just another neighbor.

Unhinged Habits

This isn't cynical; it's reality. We're all simultaneously somebody and nobody, depending on where we stand.

In his book, *The 5 Types of Wealth*, the author Sahil Bloom has a three-step framework called the New Opportunity Test that I've found useful in evaluating professional opportunities:

1. **Alignment with Priorities:** Determine if the opportunity aligns with your professional priorities. If not, decline it.
2. **"Hell Yeah!" Factor:** Assess your enthusiasm; if it's not a "Hell yeah!" response, it's a no.
3. **Realistic Expectations:** Assume the opportunity will take twice as long and be half as rewarding as expected.

If the opportunity is still appealing under these rigorous conditions, proceed.

That's the professional side though. On the personal side, no matter who you are, I've found that it really pays to say yes unless you've got a solid reason to say no.

Let me tell you how Alison and I bought our house. Toronto's a competitive market. We'd been putting bids on houses for two years. She and I went so far as to rent in three different neighborhoods to experience living there before buying. Had a checklist. The whole thing.

Finally, we found a house. It was small and old, but we decided we wanted it. Good area. Good schools. Easy walk to shops. Check, check, check. After two visits, we decided to aggressively bid. In Toronto, that means offering a lot over the asking price. No conditions. Huge deposit.

Calvin was a baby. He was still asleep in the car after our second visit to the house we planned to buy. Alison said, "You know, there's one more house. It's not in any of the areas we've been looking in. I don't know anything about the community or schools. But it's close to your family. Should we go see?" I said yes.

We drive up and see the huge trees and big lawn. Then Alison and I walk in. I go upstairs; she checks out the kitchen. After two minutes we met up and did the thing where neither of us wanted to speak first. Finally I said, "This is it." She smiled. "Yeah. This is it." Serendipity. Impossible to describe.

One of those when-you-know-you-know type things. I called Mom and Dad. They walked over. Dad looked at his watch and said, "Took us six minutes and forty-nine seconds." Mom looked at me, and said, "This is it."

We planned for two years. Knew our financial situation. Tested living in three different areas. Researched schools and walkability scores. And, at the end, none of that mattered because Calvin still happened to be sleeping in the car, and so Alison and I said yes to checking out a random house, which has become our perfect home.

What holds us back from embracing more serendipity?

It's often our misperception of risk.

Most decisions in life are framed incorrectly. We treat small choices with the same weightiness as permanent ones. And most decisions are small. To break this pattern, we need a better framework for understanding which choices are consequential and which aren't.

HATS, HAIRCUTS, AND TATTOOS

I don't like restaurants. I don't like the pomp of them. I don't like sitting down or menus or being served. And I especially don't like the feeling of ordering a full meal and not liking my food and wishing I ordered something else.

There's a framework for decision-making I originally heard from the author James Clear. It's called hats, haircuts, and tattoos. A restaurant's like a haircut. Once you go in, you're stuck with it for a while, even if you don't like it. Other decisions are like tattoos, hard to reverse out of, or hats, easy to try on and take off.

Cafés are different. Food trucks, snack bars, and walk-up windows are different; there's less commitment. You're allowed to order a little and if you like it order more. With a café, you can walk in, take a look around, taste a thing or two, and if you don't like it leave. I like cafés because, like a hat, I can try it out and if I don't like it take it off.

Most experiences you say yes to are merely hats to try on, yet you treat them like permanent tattoos—methodically overcompensating with a decision-making and fear-feeling process that's too slow, too deliberate, and too choosy, not because it's the smart thing to do but because you're scared at what might happen because you've never stopped to consider what's the worst thing that *could* happen.

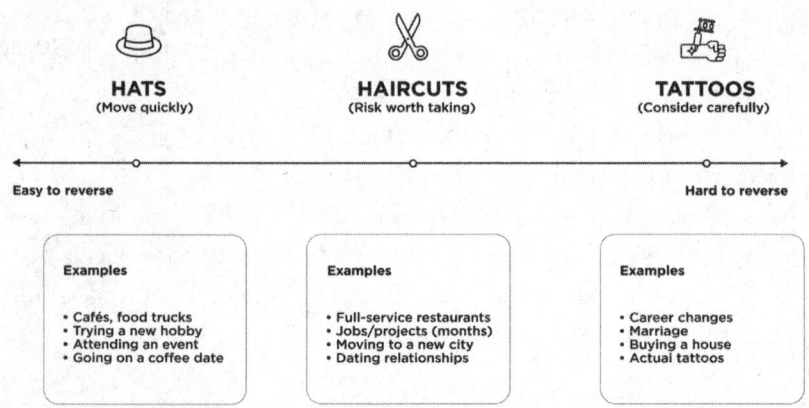

If the outcome risk is low, you can move quickly and try a lot of things. The harder the outcome is to reverse, the more energy, thought, and preparation should be used. (©Unhinged Habits)

Some decisions can represent different ends of the spectrum simultaneously. For example, buying a house is a tattoo. Alison and I had a deep understanding of our financials and nonnegotiables. Visiting one more open house, on the other hand, was a hat.

Humans being scared of the unknown is nothing new, of course. And you're not alone. There's a line I remember reading from the Stoic philosopher Seneca that made the difference for me. Helped me understand this better. Gave me more permission to do stuff.

Seneca said, "If you wish to stave off all fear, imagine that the worst that can happen most definitely will happen."

His advice was to imagine the worst-case scenario. Define your fears. If everything that could go wrong does go wrong if you say yes to a thing, what would happen? Like, what are you scared of?

You'll either realize that what you're worrying about isn't a big deal, or you'll realize it is. If the worst-case scenario is actually bad, it'll require a more deliberate decision-making process. That's all.

Whatever you want to try, consider, is it a hat, haircut, or tattoo?

I read an essay by a seventy-eight-year-old man a while back. Wish I remembered his name. Here's a line I wrote down from it: "The lesson I learned is that it really pays to say yes, unless you've got a really solid reason to say no. As I got older and lived longer, I didn't really say no. I agreed to do things. It wasn't all fun, all the time, but it often led to something interesting."

I like that.

When you recognize that most opportunities are just hats you can try on, it opens you to periods of intentional exploration.

SEASONS OF YES

I met Bruce playing pickleball in Mexico. He's an English professor who took a sabbatical in 2020 during COVID-19 and turned it into a retirement.

All I could think was that this guy looks forty, is probably in his sixties, is barefoot, and is kicking my dinking butt. *This guy has clearly figured some stuff out,* I thought.

We had a three-hour juice the next day. He told me he lived the esteemed professor life in Seattle—complete with an office with mahogany shelves and a view of the world-famous Space Needle.

"When I decided to stay here, I decided that, for the next month, I'm going to say yes to everything," he told me.

Bruce played his first pickleball game that first month. He now plays six times a week. He got involved in local charities, made new friends. There were other things he tried too that he didn't connect with. Which is fine.

By the end of the month, Bruce built a new life in a new place—renewed and refreshed, opening up a side of him he didn't know existed, just because, for thirty days, he said yes.

Seasons of Yes are powerful ways to break out of routine. They're deliberate, time-limited periods, where you commit to saying yes to opportunities, invitations, and experiences you'd normally decline.

It's not about reckless abandonment of boundaries but rather a strategic expansion of your comfort zone to break entrenched patterns and discover new possibilities. Like Bruce, many people find that this temporary change in default response opens doors they didn't know existed.

Of course, when I share this concept with people, I often see them physically recoil. The thought of saying yes more often triggers immediate concerns.

You might be having some of these reactions yourself right now. Like Michael, a forty-two-year-old tech executive who can be loosely categorized as an overwhelmed achiever. Already drowning in commitments, Michael's concern was that saying yes to more things sounded like a recipe for burnout, not discovery.

"You're not saying yes forever—you're saying yes for thirty days to break patterns," I told him. "Think of it as a short-term investment for long-term clarity. The most overwhelmed people often benefit most because they've optimized themselves into a corner."

Or there's Elena, a thirty-eight-year-old mother of two who runs a small coaching business from home. She's worked hard to establish healthy boundaries and was worried that saying yes would invite people to take advantage of her time and energy again.

"A Season of Yes isn't about saying yes to exploitation or unhealthy relationships. It's about saying yes to experiences that expand your world, not drain it," I told her.

Then I continued.

"The key is distinguishing between requests that come from others' agendas versus opportunities for genuine exploration. This is why the framework matters—you're not saying yes indiscriminately; you're saying yes strategically to things that might bring unexpected joy or learning."

Specifically, Seasons of Yes work well for four types of people:

1. **If you're professionally stuck,** have achieved some success, are trapped in a routine, and feel like you're in a comfortable rut experiencing decreased enthusiasm for your work.
2. **If you're going through a life transition,** experiencing major life changes and need to rebuild or reimagine your identity and community.

3. **If you're overly optimized** and have become so focused on efficiency and productivity that you've engineered serendipity out of your life—rarely experiencing unexpected joy or discovery, wondering "is this all there is" despite checking all of your achievement boxes.
4. **If you're seeking identity,** either earlier on in your journey as a recent graduate or going through a major career transition.

Checking in by checking out doesn't require disruptive behavior or travel. It can be done weekly, or even daily. Here's a few specific ways for you to embark on your first Season of Yes:

For the professionally stuck
- **The cross-pollination challenge:** Invest fifteen minutes daily for a month reading something completely unrelated to your industry.
- **Skills rotation:** Identify three skills adjacent to your expertise that you've never developed. Invest ten days focused on each one. Take a course; hire a coach.
- **The colleague lottery:** Randomly select one colleague each week (use a randomizer app) for a month with whom you'll have lunch or coffee. Ask specifically about their projects, approaches, and perspectives you wouldn't normally encounter.

For the life transitioners
- **The 5x5x5 community-building challenge:** For five weeks, attend five different community events or groups, and follow up with five people you meet.
- **Identity experimentation month:** Try one new activity each week that you'd never have considered part of your identity before. Document how it feels to be a "runner," "painter," "volunteer," or "chess player" even if temporarily.

Unhinged Habits

- **Daily neighborhood microadventures:** For thirty days, take a twenty-minute walk in a different direction from your home each day. Enter any public establishment that catches your interest, even if just for five minutes.

For the overly optimized
- **Practice inefficiency:** Choose one thing daily that you've optimized for efficiency and deliberately do it the "long way" for thirty days. Take the scenic route. Cook from scratch. Write by hand instead of typing.
- **The curiosity journal experiment:** Each morning for thirty days, write down three things you're curious about. Before bed, spend fifteen minutes learning about one of them.
- **The deliberate detour policy:** For thirty days, whenever you notice something interesting on your way somewhere (a new shop, a community event, an interesting person), take the detour and explore for at least fifteen minutes. Keep track of what these unplanned detours lead to.

For the identity seekers
- **The childhood passions revival:** Make a list of activities you loved as a child before external expectations took over. Spend one week reconnecting with each forgotten interest.
- **The shadow career exploration:** Identify three careers you've secretly wondered about. Designate two weeks for each and arrange coffee chats with at least five people in each of those fields and ask what their daily reality is actually like.
- **Values clarification project:** Over the course of thirteen days, interview five people whose lives you admire. Ask specific questions about how they made decisions that shaped their path, then reflect on which approaches resonate with you.

Make More Mistakes

For more ideas and inspiration, you can download fifteen additional examples of Seasons of Yes at www.Jonathangoodman.com/yes.

Alice Lemée is the last person I want to tell you about. She grew up in Brooklyn and fell out of love with NYC. She wanted to get out. She wanted to surf more and explore more and see the world more. But she met a guy, and they fell in love and so she stayed in New York.

On a day where she felt particularly burned out, Alice asked herself a challenging question:

"Is love enough to compensate for not becoming the person I wanted to be before this relationship?"

"No," she decided.

So she broke up with the dude and left for Canggu, a surfing resort town in the south of Bali.

After four months, Alice decided that she still loved the guy, and he still loved her, and it was time to come home.

She'd grown and evolved, but the city she returned to was the same. Stepping back into the same routines would just burn her out again.

Alice needed to make New York a city she could exist within.

And so she decided that the summer of 2024 was going to be her "Summer of Yes."

She wrote a post on X about it in June. I saw her post and saved the link to it in my notes. Then, on August 1, when I was ready to start this chapter, I sent her a message:

Unhinged Habits

Alice. Hey!

I had saved your post about the "Say Yes Season" from a while back and would love to know more about it. Specifically, I'd love to know more about the impetus behind your season, any emotions related to it, and how it's going.

Free for a walking chat on the phone?

She responded soon after:

"Hey Jonathan! This is super cool (and oh so very serendipitous). I'm down—it is the Summer of Yes after all. :)"

She's near the end of her Summer of Yes. It expanded her social network and brought her tremendous professional opportunities—new freelance writing gigs and online mentions from people she met that has led to thousands of email subscribers.

Most of all though, she now feels like New York is a place she can exist within, evolved, as the person she's become, not as she was. There's more to Alice's love story. I'm looking forward to telling you more about her later in the book.

Seasons of Yes are disruptive by design. They're not easy, and you can't do them often. If you're feeling stuck right now, maybe give one a try.

By now you might be wondering, "How can I embrace the rigid seasonal focus from chapter 2 and the spontaneous serendipity here?"

This apparent contradiction is actually a powerful complementary relationship. Think of it like breathing: you need both the inhale (structure) and exhale (spontaneity) for a complete breath.

Here's when each approach works best:

Default to Structure When:
- You're pursuing a specific, measurable goal with a deadline.
- You're developing a new skill that requires consistent practice.
- You're feeling scattered across too many commitments with little progress on any.

- You've identified a priority that needs breakthrough progress, not incremental improvement.

Default to Spontaneity When:
- You're between intense seasons and need renewal before the next focus.
- You're feeling stuck in rigid patterns that no longer serve you.
- You're seeking new inspiration, connections, or perspectives.
- You've completed a significant project and need to refill your cup.

The magic lies not in choosing one over the other but in understanding when to shift gears. Structure creates the container that makes meaningful spontaneity possible. Spontaneity provides the raw material that makes structured seasons productive.

Without seasons of intense focus, spontaneity becomes aimless wandering. Without periods of openness, structured seasons become rigid and depleting.

This is why an unhinged approach works: it acknowledges both needs and gives each its proper time and place. Like the natural in/out rhythm of a breath.

While individual exploration through Seasons of Yes helps us break out of personal ruts, there's another powerful way to check in by checking out—one that connects us with others rather than sending us on solo adventures.

COLLECTIVE RESTORATION

I know a thirty-two-year-old small-business owner with five kids who reads a novel a week.

Reading for pleasure is wonderful. I want to do it more but don't give myself permission. Whenever I'm reading fiction I feel guilty that I'm not reading nonfiction. Or that I'm not doing some other sort of self-development, crossing off an item on my to-do list, or, or, or.

How does this guy make the time to read?

Unhinged Habits

He's orthodox Jewish and observes Shabbat, Judaism's day of rest.

Every week, Friday to Saturday, sundown to sundown, he checks out of his life and reads a novel.

Okay, I'm about to talk about religion now. Throughout this book I'm going to be talking about a few different gods and a few different religions.

Please don't let the mention of God distract you from a good idea. I'm not religious. If you are and God works for you, great. If you're not, think of God as a rebranded version of the human collective. The greater "We." The underlying connective tissue that connects us.

No matter what you believe, or don't believe, you have to accept one fundamental truth: religion, energetics, and spirituality are all different brandings of the same idea—and that idea is the most powerful force on earth. That idea has outlasted every civilization and grown, not shrunk, with technological progress. Call it whatever you want, brand it however you want—it matters.

At its core, every religion attempts to do the same thing: explain the unexplainable, provide guidelines for how to be a good person, and give lessons on how to live a good life. The lessons themselves have value, devoid of their connection to a deity. So take the aspects that serve you and leave the rest. Drink the soup, spit the bones.

For the past six winters, my home has been the pueblo of Sayulita in Mexico. In total, I've lived there almost two full years of my life.

Something I got used to when I started going there was that on Sunday everything was closed. Nobody worked. Stores were shut. Restaurants didn't serve. And cleaners didn't clean.

It was a day off together—the Sabbath.

Sadly, it's not like that anymore. Tourism's become too profitable. The pressure from the wealthy business owners to make as much money as possible became too great.

The American Presbyterian minister Eugene Peterson calls whatever Sunday has turned into in Western culture the "bastard Sabbath," the illegitimate child of the seventh day. Sunday used to be a day of rest. Now it's just kind of a day to deal with all the shit you let pile up the rest of your week.

There was this Swedish study on happiness I heard about. The first thing it showed is that more time off made people happier. That's obvious, I guess, despite more than 55 percent of people in the United States not using all their paid time off.

What the study also showed is that synchronized time off—collective restoration—makes the entire country of Sweden happier, including even retirees, despite their not having jobs.

"It's not hard to guess why collective restoration is so powerful," writes Oliver Burkeman in *The Guardian*. "It's easier to nurture relationships with family and friends when they're on leave, too; meanwhile, if the office is deserted while you're trying to relax, you're spared anxious thoughts about tasks piling up, inboxes filling, or scheming colleagues trying to steal your job."

The Swedes practice a daily tradition called *fika*. It's a moment to slow down and appreciate the good things in life—emphasizing relaxation and connection with friends, family, or colleagues. Everybody enjoys a coffee and cake break at the same time. Many Swedish companies build two fifteen-minute *fika* breaks into their days, often at 10:00 a.m. and 3:00 p.m., though the timing varies. The point is that it's a company-wide break.

So this isn't about the Sabbath specifically. What my fiction-reading friend told me is that Shabbat isn't valuable because some ancient scroll says that it is.

"The idea of a Sabbath has persisted not just because a day off is good, but because it's the same day off for everyone," wrote Judith Shulevitz in her book *The Sabbath World*.

Shabbat is valuable because it shatters mindless workaholism and the inability to recognize the blessings of rest, reflection, spirit, and family.

Shabbat is valuable because it's an act of renewal.

Shabbat is valuable because it recognizes that community depends on synchronicity.

This isn't about God, whoever your God(s) may or may not be. It doesn't need religious undertones. Whether it's a Saturday, Sunday, Tuesday, or even weekly—none of that matters.

Unhinged Habits

The word *Shabbat* literally means "to stop." "The Sabbath is simply a day to stop: stop working, stop wanting, stop worrying, just stop," wrote John Mark Comer in *The Ruthless Elimination of Hurry*.

Alison and I don't have a name for our day. It's usually Sunday, though not always.

We don't set our alarms, and when we wake up, nobody reaches for their phones. I grab a book, she picks up her knitting or crafting, and we sit on the couch or patio.

The kids slowly make their way downstairs and because the parents aren't zapped into their screens and we've strategically left out books and toys, they take their cue and join us.

I'm writing this like it's peaceful. It's not, obviously.

My kids are two and seven. Peace exists only in thirty-second spurts. But that's what we signed up for. And using the words of the two old Eastern European ladies who saw us carrying our stroller up the stairs at a subway station while my older son was crying because he scraped his knee, we're going to look back and say, "Those were the best days of our lives."

Our rules aren't written down anywhere. Unlike observant Jews, we use electricity and drive places—but when we do, it's to see friends, not run errands.

"Friday nights it's really important to sit back, enjoy, smile, you know, give your kids a kiss, and think about how fortunate we are. And really appreciate your life," says David Segal, cofounder of *David's Tea*.

Segal continued, "Monday comes around; it's like you're at war. You're in the trenches. You're driving hard. I'm trying to build. I'm trying to build companies. My wife will always say, 'Isn't there something good going on?' And there is. The good comes on Friday night."

Sabbath gets roped in with religion. And that works for some people. But because of its religious association, others get immediately turned off when they hear the words *God*, *Shabbat*, or *Sabbath*. Brand it however you want. All that matters is that we've lost touch with this great tradition.

Whatever fire is going on in the business can wait a day. Whatever errand needs to be run can be put off. And whatever chaos in the world people are upset about right now on the internet can be ignored.

I write this acknowledging my privilege. Not everybody has the luxury to check out on Sunday. But you might be surprised what happens when you commit to a practice like this. Remember my friend? The orthodox Jewish guy with five kids? He's not rich. His entire family shares two bedrooms on one rented floor of a house.

"What I've noticed," he told me, "is that Shabbat forces me to be more structured throughout the week. Instead of Saturday being a throwaway day to get stuff done I don't feel like doing the rest of the week, it's a day I look forward to. Knowing that we have the day to rest, my wife and I are more diligent about making sure errands are run and the fridge is stocked."

Before we move on, I want to leave you with a few questions to consider when planning your collective restoration:

PLANNING FOR COLLECTIVE RESTORATION

Step 1: Identify your needs

Who do I want to spend more quality time with?

_____
_____

How much time do I realistically need to feel restored?

_____
_____

Step 2: Find your restoration partners

Who would benefit from regular restoration time with me?

_____

What mutual interests or needs do I share with them?

_____

Unhinged Habits

What might prevent them from participating?

_____

_____

Step 3: Design your rhythm

Weekly restoration block (two to twenty-four hours):

_____

_____

Monthly deeper restoration (half day to full weekend):

_____

_____

Who needs to agree to make this happen?

_____

_____

Step 4: Make it an agreement

We will protect these times from interruption by:

_____

_____

Our collective restoration will start on (date): _____

We will communicate about scheduling changes by:

_____

_____

We will review how this is working every _____ weeks / months.

Step 5: Boundaries

What will we say no to during restoration time?
_____
_____

What technology boundaries will we set?
_____
_____

You can download your own copy of this Collective Restoration worksheet at www.Jonathangoodman.com/restore.

Serendipity and productivity oppose one another. If you feel like you're in a rut, decide on a season to say yes. You'll get less done. And it will be wonderful.

Checking in requires checking out. Of the routines that trap you. Of the certainty that blinds you. Of the productivity that empties you.

I can't help but think of Plato's cave right now.

The parable is about prisoners, chained in a cave in a way that they can only look straight ahead at a wall.

There's a fire between them and people carrying stuff like vases. The prisoners can't turn around, so all that they see are shadows on the wall.

Shadow puppets, basically. And it's all that they know.

Unhinged Habits

Then one prisoner gets free.

At first, the sun blinds him. Everything hurts. He wants to go back to the comfort of the cave. To the shadows. But he stays. His eyes adjust. And holy shit, he sees actual trees. And stars.

He runs back to tell his friends. They think he's gone mad. All they know are shadows. All they've ever known are shadows.

We're those prisoners. Our chains are our narrow bands of knowledge. The shadows we see are our routines that we accept as normal, if only by our acquiescence to them.

Seasons of Yes are a way to break out of the cave. Collective restoration are moments when we stop to truly see. The first for checking out, the second for checking back in.

The world outside your familiar shadows is wider than you can imagine. And in that wideness, you'll find both the serendipity and wonder that you crave.

So, admit what you don't know.

Say yes, even if it scares you.

And, whether it's a daily *fika*, a weekly Sabbath, or synchronized vacations, it's perhaps helpful to design a pause, together.

Now onto why you should mow your own damn lawn.

CHAPTER 3 SUMMARY

- **Create a Season of Yes.** Designate a limited period (typically thirty days) in which you deliberately say yes to experiences outside your routine. This intentional disruption breaks patterns, creates serendipity, and reveals unexpected paths.

- **Admit what you don't know.** As we age, we narrow our bands of knowledge and become trapped in our own certainty. Embrace the humility of uncertainty rather than clinging to false confidence.

- **Recognize that most decisions are "hats," not "tattoos."** Understand which choices are easily reversible (hats), somewhat reversible (haircuts), or permanent (tattoos). This framework frees you to experiment more with low-risk opportunities.

- **Synchronize your rest.** The power of traditions like Sabbath lies not in taking time off, but in taking the *same* time off as others. Create deliberate pauses with the people you love to strengthen relationships and provide the renewal that solitary rest cannot.

4.

Choose Your Hard

Worthy struggle creates energy.

I knew a guy who sold his company for a lot of money. Some medical software thing. He never shared how much it sold for. But it was enough to never need to work again. Tens of millions. Then he applied for a minimum-wage job as a caretaker for a spiritual garden.

"Your blessing in life is when you find the torture you're comfortable with," said Jerry Seinfeld. A bad job can still be good work.

There's a paradox with fitness: while working out is hard, living out of shape is harder. The same is true of mental work. Our brains, like our bodies, need the right kind of resistance to remain sharp and function at their best.

Much of our current culture celebrates escaping work, suggesting that the goal is to earn an effortless life.

But what if that's exactly backward?

What if the goal isn't to eliminate hardship but to choose the right kind of hard?

First, some stories of people who earned lots of money and prestige only to find themselves miserable, as a kind of warning shot to ground us. Next, how your attention determines your energy more than your workload does. And finally, the power of a cognitive snack for all-day energy.

This is a fun one. Might change the way you think and act. Did for me, at least. Helped me out of a funk.

Unhinged Habits

A lot of good waits for you on the other side of tired.

There's a parable about a Mexican fisherman. You've probably heard it before, but I've got a new take. It goes like this.

This fisherman's boat always had several large, fresh fish in it. An American investment banker on vacation asked the fisherman how long his catch took him.

"Only a little while," the man replied. "I have more than enough to support my family."

The American then asked what he did with the rest of his time.

"I sleep late, fish a little, play with my children, take a siesta with my wife, and stroll into the village each evening where I sip wine and play guitar with my friends."

"You should buy a bigger boat. Then you'll make more money and be able to afford a fleet of boats. And eventually you'll be able to move to the big city and open your own cannery."

The fisherman asked how long this would take.

"Fifteen to twenty years."

"Then what?"

"Then you will be rich and can retire."

"And what would I do then?"

"Then, my friend, you will have no worries. You could move to a small coastal fishing village where you would sleep late, fish a little, play with your kids, take a siesta with your wife, and stroll to the village in the evenings where you could sip wine and play your guitar with your friends."

The fisherman and banker represent two fundamentally different approaches to time and purpose. My problem with the parable is that it presents a false choice.

It assumes perpetual contentment is possible without purpose, and that purpose must be sacrificed for contentment.

I don't think either man has it right. Let's talk about this more.

"Enjoy the process." It's advice we hear all of the time. "Do the verb in order to become the noun," they say. "Relish the experience." "Savor the journey." "Cherish the adventure," you're told.

Choose Your Hard

And it's all good advice in theory. Without application though, it's useless. First, some helpful terminology. Then, a new spin on that old story.

There are two types of activities: finite and infinite.

Finite activities aim at terminal states. Getting married is finite: it's done when you're wed. Writing a book is finite: it's done when you tap the final key. Driving somewhere is finite: it's done when you arrive.

Infinite activities don't aim at a terminal state. It doesn't drive toward finishing. It describes the process. Which never completes.

The same activity done differently can be either finite or infinite. For example, walking home is finite: home is the end state. Going for an aimless walk, on the other hand, is infinite. It's true that you will eventually stop walking, but aimless walks are never completed. As a result, the two feel radically different.

In our future-focused society, we're trained to be finite. Always striving to get *there*, never *here*. Thinking about the past, driving toward the future, while leaving the present curiously unoccupied.

I live in a small Mexican fishing village most winters.

One morning at the gym, I met Isaac. A Mexican-American. He was born in town. Went to college in California. Got some finance degree. Then came back.

He works out every morning with his girlfriend and dog.

At sunset, you'll find him playing Spikeball on the beach with friends.

During the day he works at the best taco spot in town.

I've never seen Isaac without a smile. He's fit, eats fresh fruit, gets free tacos, and is surrounded by people that he loves.

But a part of me also knows that I wouldn't be able to do what he does. And I also wonder how long he'll be able to do it.

It's too perfect.

Idyllic days on repeat where the sun shines, the food's delicious, and the activities are great are nice in theory. Without contrast, however, desensitization sets in, and it leads to burnout just the same.

Unhinged Habits

There needs to be something to work toward. Just catching fish, even if you aim to get a bit better at it each day, isn't enough.

And so, I'm left with a paradox. Call it the false allure of early retirement. Of giving the middle finger to the real world and replacing it with beautifully perfect days on repeat: the problem with the Mexican fisherman story.

On one hand, a project-driven life is no way to live. On the other hand, there's also no way to live other than to be driven by projects.

We obviously shouldn't wait to retire to buy a sailboat and sail around the world. Maybe we won't ever be able to afford it. Or something tragic happens and we die. Or maybe we'll finally make it to those golden years and buy a sailboat only to discover that sailing sucks. Or that golf becomes horrendously boring when you do it more than three times a year.

Here's my challenge.

I want to fall in love with the process and ignore the outcome. But I can't. I just can't. I'm always thinking about the outcome. Want to know what I'm thinking right now? This second. At 11:25 a.m. on October 28, 2024. As I type these words. I'm thinking, *Will this book succeed? Will it sell? Will anybody care?*

I once produced three books. I say produced because even though my name is on them, I didn't write them. The books made some money. Not a lot. Enough to be a good business decision. But I learned nothing from the experience. I gained nothing from the experience.

I don't care about those books enough to even display them on my shelf. They mean nothing to me. They did nothing for me. Purely finite. A strategic business decision. A means to an end.

We had plans to do at least five books in the series. After three I said enough was enough, thanked the talented ghostwriter, and paid him a severance. Then I swore that it was going to be the last time I ever did the work solely for the money. Because even though I did get some money, I got nothing from the work.

Writing this book, on the other hand, has helped me become more of the father, husband, friend, spouse, and boss that I want to be. I'm writing about being more happy, grateful, and adventurous. I'm reading and listening and thinking about those things constantly throughout the day. As a result, this work has made me more of the human that I want to be.

Your job is what you do for money. Your work is what you do for you. They say to follow your passion. And you should. But your passion should probably be your work, not your job. When you make your passion your job, you will depend on the income from it to support yourself. Which has a habit of ruining the love you have for your passion.

The week after I handed in the first draft of this book, my previous one, *The Obvious Choice,* got released. It sold well out of the gate. Met with critical acclaim. Incredibly positive reviews. Want to know what was weird? I felt sad. I never feel sad. But for the first time in my life, I felt sad. Like, I didn't want to get out of bed. That no matter how much accounting I did of everything good going on in my life, it didn't matter.

There was music and tacos and people that I love around. Despite that, my world felt gray. I lost my appetite. Was exhausted. Had a short temper with my kids. Every day, a malaise. Alison even took me to the medical clinic. The doc checked me head to toe. Didn't find anything. That's because I wasn't sick. At least, not in the traditional sense.

For three years, I had worked on *The Obvious Choice.* Then the first physical copy arrived. And I held it. Then release day came, and people bought it. And there was nothing more for me to do. The project was finished.

Alison organized a party the night of the release. Invited our friends. Had Spanish guitar music playing in the background. Got a cake made with a picture of the book. All the time I should have been soaking in the celebration and praise—happy and proud—but I felt neither of those things. Instead, an emptiness. Like, "That's it?" After that party, I lay down in bed and stayed there for three days.

The rewards you get from the outcome of any finished project are never as great as the rewards you get from the project itself. No amount of praise, prestige, or profit after the fact replaces the internal growth when you're stuck in the messy middle of something.

Unhinged Habits

It's okay to be driven by projects. Good, even. So much so, that the worst thing that can happen is that you don't have one bearing down on you.

I got out of the funk by getting back to work.

The smartest thing that I did when I finished my last book was start this one. And the smartest move I can make when I finish this one is start the next one.

When you find the right project to work on, the worst thing that can happen is that you finish it. And the first thing you should do when that happens is start the next.

Maybe that's not healthy. Maybe it's better to rest on your laurels for a bit. Soak it in. Rest. Recharge. Or maybe, the body is like a car battery in that it needs consistent movement to stay energized.

Doing work that matters is challenging. Work that matters to you, not others. That's the only litmus test.

I've got a friend who watches a movie every night after his nine-to-five job at a bank. Some middle management position at a local branch. Twice a week, he and a buddy record a podcast about obscure movie trivia. That's awesome! They even have a sponsor now. What a cool thing to work on.

He took something that he enjoys and turned it into a project to share with a friend. Now he's building a side hustle business out of it. Will it go anywhere? Don't know. Doesn't matter. He's having fun and learning new things. Audio production, selling sponsorships, communication.

Work that makes you better while you're doing the work, not for it being done, is a wonderful thing. No matter what you're working on.

But if you cannot explore within your work, no matter how big or important your work is, or how much money it makes you, you will burn out and it will feel empty.

If you finish your work and have nothing else to challenge you, no matter how big or important it is, or how much money it makes you, you will burn out and it will feel empty.

Sure, celebrate the win. Take a breath. Enjoy it. You've earned it.

But don't linger there too long.

Celebrations become hollow when extended indefinitely. Your mind needs friction; spirit craves challenge. All muscles atrophy without weight.

Choose Your Hard

FINDING THE GOOD-TIRED SWEET SPOT

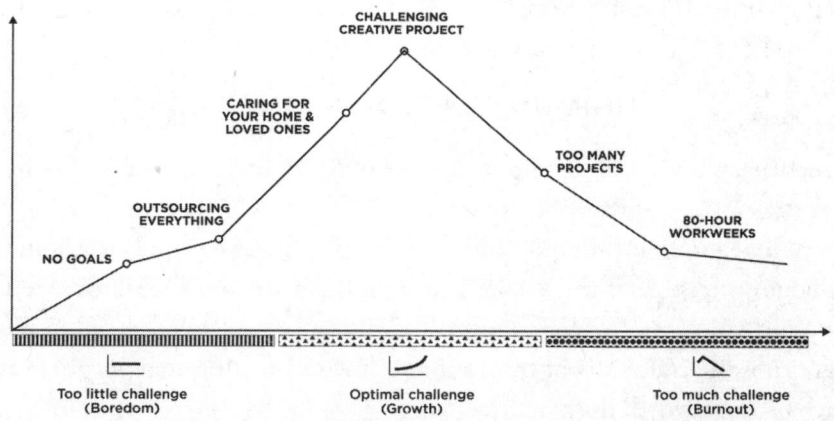

Having a single creative project in addition to doing the work involved in caring for your home and loved ones provides the optimal amount of growth and challenge. Outsourcing too much results in boredom, and taking on too many projects at once results in burnout. (©Unhinged Habits)

When it comes to money (and your job), there's such a thing as enough. We've gotta stop the goalposts of excess and desire from moving. With work, however, the moment one project finishes, find the next to drive toward. Keep those goalposts moving so long as you find the infinite within the finite.

Waking up each day in the same bed. To the same perfect weather. With the same routine. With no stress. With no challenging project forcing you to figure some shit out. To improve. It's a miserably empty existence. You need the work.

Remove all struggle, and you'll lose your way of being, lost in a heap of your own prosperity—bankrupted by a life of leisure.

I used to love the parable of the Mexican fisherman. Then I took on the task of writing this book. Which forced me to think deeper about the story. That's when I thought back to Isaac. The lesson he taught me was that the parable of the Mexican fisherman is nonsense. And maybe the American businessman isn't as crazy as he's made to appear.

"No man ever steps in the same river twice, for it's not the same river and he's not the same man," according to Heraclitus. Ending up in the same spot you started is perfectly fine so long as the circular journey to get there was fun and fulfilling, because even though the spot you ended up in is the same, you won't be.

MINIMUM-WAGE MILLIONAIRES

"Security is a kind of death," wrote the playwright Tennessee Williams in his essay "The Catastrophe of Success."

We've gotten lost in this "Hey, everybody. This is fast and easy. Join us" ridiculousness. As if the dream is to win the game, quit, chill out, retire, and put your feet up. Watch more TV, play more golf. We're told to *relax*. Ignoring the trade-offs of burnout and low satisfaction that accompany a lack of work worth doing.

It's exciting to have goals when you're young. But then, suddenly, if all goes well and reality exceeds everything you thought was possible, something very counterintuitive happens: you don't know what to hope for next.

In 2008, Mark Manson started writing online. Then, in 2015, he published a blog article called "The Subtle Art of Not Giving a F***." It went viral.

At the same time, he was working on a book, and his agent suggested a title change to match the viral blog article. The speed of the success of the book upon release was unprecedented. It exploded out of the gate, selling ten million copies, lasting more than three hundred weeks on the *New York Times* bestseller list (and counting).

He'd done it. Mark had done it. Reached the top of the mountain. The hard work had paid off. He'd made it. Plucked from obscurity into sudden prominence. Rags to riches. The American dream.

Here's what he later said about that period:

> It's like, oh, everything I had hoped for my entire adult life just happened in the last three months. And I have no idea what to do next. I have no plans beyond this point. I'm 32. So, shit. I guess I'll just order pizzas and play video games. And drink. And that's basically

what I did for most of 2017. It's actually one of the most unhealthy years of my life. Which is very strange.

Notice what happens in this story: video games, excessive drinking, physical comfort. The mind and body stagnate together. Without meaningful mental challenge, the body loses purpose. Similarly, without physical exertion, the mind loses focus.

Every hiker knows that you have to account for altitude sickness when climbing a mountain. Ascend too fast and your body and mind cannot adapt.

Many of us (including me) dream that we will win the proverbial (or actual) lottery. The reality is that you would be much better off with a slow ascent, taking breaks at the end of each switchback to catch your breath, sip some water, and enjoy the view.

You needn't study lottery winners for long to notice how ruinous winning too big and too fast can be. While not a direct parallel to Mark's story (he earned it), in many ways, a slow and gradual ascent complete with ups and downs is healthier and leads to a greater quality of life both throughout and at the top.

After months of this purposeless drift, Manson realized he needed a new mountain to climb—something that would push him beyond his comfort zone and reignite his creative drive.

YouTube represented a new challenge, one in which he could leverage some of his same skills but that also forced him to acquire new ones—learning storytelling in a new way, camera angles, lighting, and more. "I like having to claw my way back again," he said. "It's a much more comfortable position for me psychologically than feeling like I'm on top of the mountain, desperately trying to stay up there."

You'll never love 100 percent of your work. I think that's important to remember.

When you take on a difficult project, it stretches you. You get stronger. And the next time it doesn't feel so hard. Meeting your potential is a worthwhile goal to strive for. Your potential is, of course, a constantly moving goal line, impossible to cross yet still worth striving for.

Unhinged Habits

You're made to work. Without it, borrowing a phrase from Tennessee Williams, "The man is a sword cutting daisies." Your goal isn't to stop working or to escape the rat race. Your goal is to design a life filled with challenging projects you don't want to escape from.

Don't seek an easy life. Choose your hard. If you don't, it will manifest in depression and listlessness. Working makes you worth a damn, regardless of whether you get paid or how much.

Last night, with my head resting softly on my pillow, I lay awake worrying. Worrying about what, I've no idea. Nothing important. But worrying. That's what my dumb brain decided to do.

Earlier that evening, my wife and I hired a babysitter and drove to Chinatown for Yummy Yummy Dumplings and foot massages. Is it a coincidence that the only night I had trouble sleeping this week was also the only night I indulged in luxury? About as much of a coincidence that a restaurant with the audacity to include the word *yummy* twice in their title makes wicked good food.

The comfort of ease and absence of difficulty leads to anxiety. "The secret of being miserable is to have leisure to bother about whether you are happy or not. The cure for it is occupation," wrote George Bernard Shaw. When our mind is vacant, it fills with emotions. "That is why it is necessary to happiness that one should be tired," Shaw concluded.

Stress and anxiety feed on idleness. Fatigue breaks down your natural safety nets. You're less likely to lie and bullshit yourself after doing something difficult. "There are only two tragedies. One is not getting what one wants, and the other is getting it," wrote Oscar Wilde.

Struggling to pay your bills is miserable. When you're living paycheck to paycheck, the idea of "choosing your hard" might seem like a luxury you can't afford. But this is precisely when understanding this principle matters most.

Let me be clear: I'm not suggesting you should find joy in financial hardship or pretend that structural barriers don't exist. They do. And they're real. But within even the most constrained circumstances, you have a critical choice about whether you maintain your agency or allow it to be stripped from you.

Consider Maria, a single mother working two jobs to support her family. Mornings at a warehouse, evenings waiting tables, and a precious few hours in between for her children. "Surviving," she used to tell people when they asked how she was doing.

"I don't have the luxury of choosing anything," she told me. "I take whatever work I can get."

Maria's external circumstances didn't initially change. What changed was her relationship to the job she had to do anyway.

Rather than seeing her warehouse job as mindless labor, she treated the physical movement as her daily exercise. Her "worthy struggle," she now calls it. She started timing herself, tracking steps. Thinking of manual labor as exercise you get paid to do was a wonderful rebrand.

At her evening restaurant job, she began studying the operation as if she were preparing to run her own business someday. She began paying attention to customer patterns, management decisions, and service efficiencies.

This shift in mindset created small moments of agency within her job that had previously felt like pure obligation. The physical tiredness remained, but the mental and emotional exhaustion began to lift. She was choosing her hard.

This approach didn't erase her financial challenges. But it did create more mental and emotional bandwidth for her to take a distance-study class in bookkeeping, which led to a better paying position within the restaurant group she used to wait tables for.

Maria's story isn't about magical thinking—it's about reclaiming agency where possible. Mindset alone doesn't solve structural differences. Class divides unfairly exist. Still, choosing how you engage with difficulty creates space for possibility where none existed before.

Her story reminded me of a manager I didn't like early on in my personal training days. For the time being, I was stuck there—though I knew that wouldn't last. It couldn't. I wouldn't allow it. So I started a folder on my computer called "thoughts on management." Nobody knew.

Instead of getting frustrated when I'd get mistreated, I used it as fodder for study. I didn't know it at the time, but I was reclaiming agency. Each nasty interaction became energizing, not demoralizing. An opportunity to learn.

Here are a few choices you get to make, regardless of the hand you were dealt:

- **Approach versus avoidance:** You can fully engage with necessary work or mentally check out while doing it.
- **Growth versus stagnation:** You can look for learning opportunities within constraints or simply endure them.
- **Connection versus isolation:** You can build relationships within difficult circumstances or withdraw into private suffering.

None of these choices eliminate hardship, but they change how hardship affects you.

When options are limited, choosing your hard might simply mean choosing to be fully present in your current struggle rather than mentally escaping it. It might mean finding a way to convert mandatory effort into something that strengthens rather than depletes you.

The wealthy person who quits a high-paying job they hate to pursue a passion project has made a visible choice. The person who transforms their relationship to a job that they cannot leave has made an equally powerful choice, albeit a less visible one.

On the other hand, if you already have enough money, congratulations, you've won that game. Now go find another one to play. Or else. Think: *What do you enjoy being bad at?* Maybe start there.

Don't avoid work. Instead, find work worth doing. How much money you make from it is one consideration. More important to some than others depending on ambition and circumstances.

Two reflection questions.

- If you had a billion dollars, what work would you do for free?
- What's one area where you're taking an "easy" route that's actually making your life harder or less fulfilling?

Choose Your Hard

MOWING LAWNS

It's 2:00 a.m. and I have to pee.

I'm in a tent. In Greenland. It's pitch-black outside. There's snow on the ground. I'm in my underwear. And I can't find my socks.

Our group was fifty miles away from another human. To get there, we left a settlement of forty-eight people, took an hour boat ride, and hiked five hours.

When you do hard things alongside others, you get close to them.

Our comfortable modern lives often miss the connection from shared challenges.

The strongest bonds aren't formed over drinks at a resort. They're forged in mutual struggle.

We've engineered hardship out of our lives. Then we wonder why we feel so disconnected. Our ancestors didn't schedule "connection time." They hunted together. Built stuff together. Survived long winters together.

When you eliminate the hard parts of life, you eliminate the glue that holds people together.

I used to hire a company to mow my lawn for me. For the first two years I lived in my home, I decided that my time was worth more than what it would cost to hire out the job.

Then, one day, I mowed my own lawn.

And I felt a pride in beautifying my home that surprised me.

And that's when I realized that calculating how much your time is worth and hiring out all jobs that cost less than your time value is missing the most important thing. Which is that some jobs are simply worth doing.

We still have our house cleaned once every two weeks.

My oldest son, Calvin, doesn't pick up after himself. Drives us nuts.

It's our fault, not his. He doesn't pick up after himself because we don't pick up after ourselves. That needs to change. Children don't do what you tell them to do. They do what they see you do.

I read something from the Harvard professor Clayton Christensen a while back that stuck with me. He said that he was glad that they didn't have enough money to buy a perfectly finished house when his kids were young.

Unhinged Habits

Looking back, he's grateful their house was a wreck, and they couldn't afford to pay tradesman to fix it. "Everything that needed to be fixed had to be fixed by us and by the kids. Now, most people would think of this as a complete chore. But inadvertently, we had moved our family into an environment rich in opportunities for us to work together," he wrote.

I think back to my situation.

If the only consideration were money, we would pay for all of the help around the house that we'd ever need. Landscapers, cleaners, tradesmen. But depriving my kids of the opportunity to care for our home alongside us is too high a price to pay.

Alison and I decided to fill in our garden beds with stone. Three tons. The job took two months.

I'd take thirty-minute "breaks" in between podcast recordings to move stones. Then get back to my desk refreshed. Exhausting the body energizes the mind. Physical movement increases blood flow to the brain, releases mood-enhancing compounds, and seems to reset our ability to focus.

The first few times hauling stone, my boys watched. We didn't tell them that they had to help. Leadership is by doing, not demanding.

A few days in, they toddled outside to join me. They didn't help much. Honestly, they made the job harder.

I'd shovel. They'd pick up a few stones by hand and put them in the wheelbarrow. Then they'd walk beside me as I wheeled the load to its spot. After dumping the pile, they hopped inside the wheelbarrow for a ride back.

Two weeks later, I'm outside shoveling, and I see Calvin rearranging my stones in a sloping garden bed. "I'm making a wall so they don't fall. It's like building blocks," he said.

My work that day was to be his helper.

I would have never thought to build a wall along the slope. He did. It was smart. I picked through my pile to find the biggest stones and brought them to him.

His design is still there.

There's something fundamentally different about working alongside your children versus just playing with them. Play teaches children that you enjoy their company. Work teaches them that you value their contribution.

When Calvin arranged those stones, he became my collaborator. My partner. His eyes showed a new kind of pride. Not from having fun. But from seeing his ideas become real. From knowing his work mattered. To me. To our home.

Shared effort builds a different family bond. Deeper than entertainment. It creates mutual respect. There's a time for fun experiences with one another. And there's time for creating something together. Stone by stone.

And so, I propose a new way of thinking about housework. One that takes into account time and money, of course. But also one that accounts for the loss in the joy of the work, the loss of the pride of having done the work, and the loss in connection to your children formed as a result of the work.

When deciding which tasks to do yourself versus outsource, consider the four *work-worth-doing tests*:

The Connection Test: Will this help me build meaningful relationships?

Making dinner with your spouse might take longer than takeout. Efficiency isn't the point. Chatting while chopping veggies is the point.

The Growth Test: Will this teach me something valuable?

Building that bookshelf might take you three times longer than a professional, but the skills and confidence you gain might serve you for decades.

The Pride Test: Will being able to say "I did that" bring me genuine satisfaction?

Many achievements feel hollow when purchased rather than earned.

The Legacy Test: Will this create memories to pass down?

Teaching your child to change a tire might seem inefficient compared to calling roadside assistance, but you're doing it together, passing down a skill.

Work worth delegating usually fails these tests.

When we think about which tasks to do ourselves and which to delegate, most people use a simple calculation: "Is my time worth more than what I'd pay someone else to do this?"

But this misses something essential.
Some tasks have hidden value beyond efficiency.

THE WORK-WORTH-DOING TEST

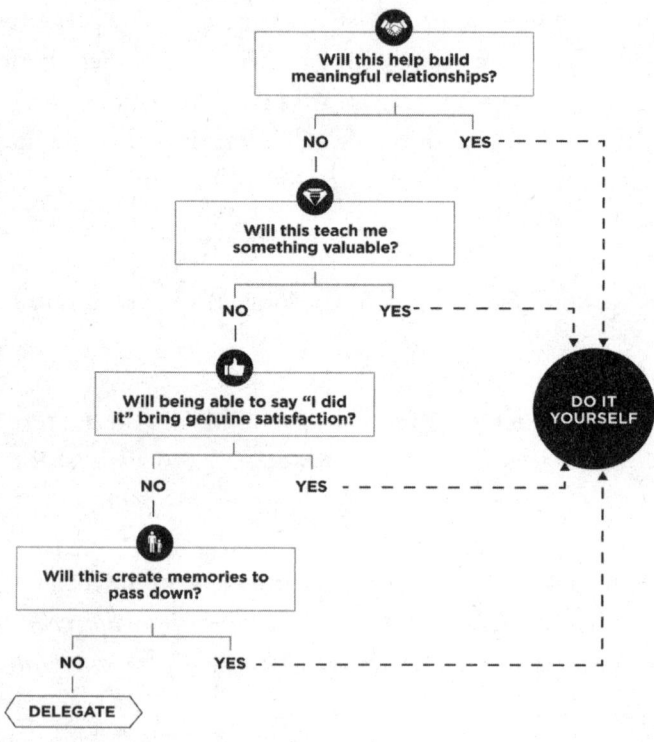

When deciding what work to do yourself versus delegate, it is valuable to consider connection, growth, pride, and legacy in addition to your time value. (©Unhinged Habits)

There's a difference between winning the Olympics versus ordering an Olympic gold medal off eBay and putting it on yourself. When you hire work to be done, it loses its meaning. It's there. The result of it is there. But it's empty. No memories. It's just another thing that exists.

I don't always like mowing my lawn. And sometimes I don't have the time.

My boys see me mowing and want to help. I'm deep into a podcast. Don't want to be bothered. This was supposed to be my time. They'll ask for a piggyback. Or want to stand between my legs and help me push the mower, hand-over-hand. All of this is a pain. It makes the job slower and harder. I don't like it. But once the job is done, I'm happy it happened.

Sometimes I'll come home and stare at my lawn. I'll smell the fresh grass clippings. On those days, I naturally end up looking at the spot where I had a boy on my back pushing the mower. The spot is no different to anybody else. To me though, that's the best damn part of my lawn.

COGNITIVE SNACKS

There are days when my brain works well. And there are days when my brain does not work well.

On good days, I finish work and have lots of energy and attention for my children. I can sit with them on the floor and play Lego, clean up after dinner, and reread them the same book about Batpig "just one more time" (five times) before falling asleep.

On bad days, I'm irritable and impatient. My body feels heavy, and my brain feels foggy. I hate how I feel, and I hate how I act toward the people that I love.

The difference between good days and bad days isn't in the amount of work that you get done, the time it took, the pressure you're under, the responsibility placed upon you, or the difficulty of your tasks. The difference between good days and bad days comes down to how well you keep your attention span focused.

Blame the algorithm or your phone's notifications as much as you want. They aren't the problem, you are. Without them, you'd still distract yourself. You're just as likely to interrupt yourself as you are to be interrupted by a notification.

Dr. Gloria Mark's done research into all of this. She wrote a book called *Attention Span*. It's worth reading.

She describes the problem of attention like this: Your brain has a blueprint for everything that you do. Some of these blueprints are simple (wash the dishes) and some are complex (navigate an HR crisis at work). Every time that you start something new, you're asking your brain to boot up the mental schema for that task.

Unhinged Habits

Energetically, pulling up a blueprint is taxing. Do it too much, too often, and too quickly, and it causes stress.

It's okay to be tired at the end of the day. What you don't want to feel is exhaustion. Exhaustion isn't the result of working harder or longer. You feel exhausted when you switch tasks too much. Working worse, you could say.

Multitasking is a myth. You are not good at it. Nobody is good at it. Nobody can do two things at once. It is a literal impossibility. The only thing that creates the illusion of multitasking is if one of the things you're doing uses automatic attention.

For example, say you're driving on a mostly empty freeway and talking to a passenger. You're doing two things: driving and talking. The driving is automatic, your conversation is not.

All of a sudden a car swerves in front of you. The driving isn't automatic anymore. It requires your attention. What happens? You stop your conversation.

If both tasks involve controlled processing, you're not multitasking. You're switching your attention back and forth.

Maya Angelou used to refer to her brain as big mind / little mind. Her big mind was used for writing. Her little mind was used for playing crossword puzzles. "People are happiest when they take cognitive snacks," says Dr. Mark. Cognitive snacks. I like that.

We're not taught how to restore constructively. Getting distracted and finding useful diversions are different things. One is good, the other is not.

It's fall right now. I'm looking out my window at the leaves falling, allowing my mind to wander instead of clicking onto social media, looking forward to my fifteen-minute break when I'm going to rake and bag some leaves—work that I could easily pay somebody else to do, but giving up the cognitive snack is too high a price to pay.

Planning easy and mindless pleasures throughout the day can be quite useful. The stuff people call a waste of time: watching a video, killing zombies, doing sudoku, all can be quite useful.

I've found that different people benefit from different types of cognitive snacks. Personally, I like physical ones. You may be different.

Here are six different ways to restore yourself constructively throughout the day:

1. **Physical snacks:** Cleaning dishes, light gardening, walking the dog, stretching.
2. **Nature snacks:** Leaning against a tree, finding shapes in clouds, listening to the birds.
3. **Analog game snacks:** Crosswords, sudoku, puzzles.
4. **Digital game snacks:** Scrolling social media, killing zombies, Candy Crush.
5. **Creative microactivity snacks:** Doodling, plucking away on a ukulele, writing a haiku.
6. **Mindfulness exercise snacks:** Deep breathing, body scanning, counting breath.

For the newly remote, this problem is even worse. The corporate office had natural breaks built in. Walking to the conference room. Small talk at the water cooler. The elevator ride. Your home doesn't. Your commute is now three steps to your desk. Your conference room is a click away. There's no break. Switching from one task to the next. Always switching.

The physical world provided natural cognitive snacks. Now you must create them.

If you work online, try the "meeting margin" rule. End every virtual meeting five minutes early. Use those five minutes to stand, stretch, look out a window. Better yet, schedule twenty-five-minute meetings instead of thirty. Or fifty instead of sixty. Or take the lead from Alex Wieckowski and add a "commute" to work, even if you work remotely, by going for a ten-to fifteen-minute walk every morning before sitting down at your desk.

Create physical distance where digital distance doesn't exist.

When you finish a task, physically move away from your desk. Even just to walk in a circle. Your brain needs a rest.

If you have the luxury, design your home workspace with multiple stations. The kitchen table for email. The desk for focused work. The couch for reading. Movement between spaces gives your brain the transition it craves.

Take breaks.

But take the right kind of breaks.

Unhinged Habits

Games are good. So is light and mindless physical work like emptying the dishwasher.

Just don't get stuck down the rabbit hole of addictive technology.

Set an alarm for ten minutes or twenty minutes or whatever. Calm yourself down with something automatic, enjoy it, and then get back to your task again.

These brief mental breaks refresh your focus. But for all-day energy, you need something more. You've gotta move. Your brain depends on your body.

PUTTING THE OX IN THE PLOW

Your brain is software. Upgrade it by reading books, learning new skills, and exploring new ideas.

Your body is hardware. Upgrade it with a physical discipline: Run, lift, bike, do Pilates; it doesn't matter.

I'm very happy I started weightlifting when I was fifteen. But the reason why I started (teenage hormones) is different from the many reasons I've continued all these years. At first, it was for mental health. Physical exertion improves my mood. Then, in my thirties, I began to see a divide among my friends. Those who didn't exercise regularly seemed to be aging quicker and getting sick more often.

Recently, I've figured out perhaps the biggest benefit of having a regular physical practice. I expect this is the one that will keep me exercising the rest of my life.

When I've exhausted my body, my brain focuses and I'm able to write better.

You're designed for physical tasks. The body is powerful. It needs to work. Devoid of physical work in a too-easy existence, your brain resorts to stress. It gets distracted, feels anxious, and lacks focus. "You got to put the ox in the plow, make it do stuff it doesn't want to do," said Jerry Seinfeld, who famously works out six days a week even though he hates it. "I just think it's very balancing to the forces inside humanity that I think just overwhelm us," he added.

Choose Your Hard

Improvements in health, longevity, and disease prevention in addition to the obvious increase in sexification aside, a strenuous physical discipline is necessary for mental achievement.

Mental work is taxing. So is sitting for extended periods of time. It's simple, really: If you want to be able to do good work for years, you've got to be physically strong. The only way to achieve the rare combination of discipline and energy for ongoing mental work is to tire yourself physically.

But there's such a thing as too much.

Last year, I attended an event in Ojai, California, with 160 others. All multimillionaires. All successful in business.

Two things stuck out to me. The first was that nobody was overweight. The second was that nobody was in noticeably ridiculously great shape. Everybody, it seemed, had stumbled upon the same truth: keeping the body fit is integral for good work, but there is a point of diminishing returns.

If I get too into my workouts, they cut into my writing time. If I go too hard, my body gets too tired and hurts for a day or two, causing distracting physical discomfort.

In their paper *Too Much of a Good Thing*, Adam Grant and Barry Schwartz reveal the inverted-U-shaped relationship—Aristotle's golden mean—between nearly everything of consequence. "All positive traits, states, and experiences have costs that at high levels begin to outweigh their benefits," they wrote.

There's a balance. Exercise and eat well so that it adds to your life, but not so much that it begins to subtract from it.

In another paper, called *The Goldilocks Zone for Exercise*, a team of cardiologists wrote that exercise can be thought of as a medicine. "As with any powerful drug, establishing the ideal therapeutic window is of crucial importance. An ineffectively low dose will not impart full benefits, whereas the adverse effects stemming from an excessively high dose may overshadow potential benefits and introduce detriments," they wrote.

The reason I continue to lift weights has evolved. I now do it to maintain, and improve, my physical condition in order to optimize my creative output.

Let's wrap this up. Two questions:

Unhinged Habits

What are two refreshing cognitive snacks you're going to add into your day?

1. _____

2. _____

What's a physical activity you can do to tire your body and energize your mind? When will you do it this week? (Be specific.)

_____
_____
_____
_____

Upgrading your hardware by making your body stronger is necessary for you to allow your software, your brain, to continue doing the work that it craves.

Work hard to rest well.

Tire the body to energize the mind.

The best night's sleep always comes after a hard day's work. An honest tiredness, the kind that comes when you know you've put everything you have into your day. Left it all on the field.

Every day, you face a choice.

The hard road of meaningful effort or the seemingly easy path that leads to emptiness. The work that tires your body but energizes your mind, or the comfort that leaves you restless.

Don't avoid work. Instead, find the work worth doing.

Choose your hard.

Choose meaningful work over empty leisure. Choose energizing exertion over dulling comfort. Choose focus over scattered distraction. These choices won't make your life easier, but they will make it better.

Next, a challenging conversation about insecure overachievement. But first, a quick update.

CHAPTER 4 SUMMARY

- **Find work worth doing, not work worth finishing.** Projects that transform you during their creation have more value than those pursued solely for completion or reward. The process matters more than the outcome.

- **Choose purposeful challenges over empty leisure.** Without the right kind of resistance, our minds and bodies atrophy in comfort.

- **Reserve some of the physical tasks for yourself.** Some work, like mowing your own lawn or building something alongside your children, creates connections, teaches skills, and builds pride in ways that hired help never can.

- **Physically tire your body to mentally energize your mind.** Regular physical exertion isn't just about health; it's the foundation for sustained mental performance, focus, and emotional well-being.

THE HALF-FULL CUP

October 25, 2024

It's been a bit more than a month. Today is October 25. My thirty-ninth birthday.

Some days are better than others. But Alison's been more or less bedridden for four weeks and counting.

Looking at a screen makes her sick. So does reading. And eating.

If she does something crazy like go for a short walk, she'll have to lie down when she gets home. She can't read to our boys. Instead, she opens a book so they can see the pictures and makes up a story.

The hardest part is that there's no defined end in sight.

She's ten and a half weeks pregnant. We're hoping that the start of the second trimester will mark the end of her nausea. There's no way to know.

One day she might just feel better.

Or maybe it'll be this way the entire pregnancy. Six more months.

We've no other option than to take it day by day.

Awful things happen. Loved ones get sick; business deals go sour; strings of bad luck feel endless. The question is not whether or not you will roll your ankle. It is whether or not rolling your ankle will injure you.

There's a lot of talk about resiliency these days. About fortitude and strength. And about gaining the skills to navigate the unknown. All of that is great. But it's just as important to expect the unexpected. Because the only thing you can expect to happen with any degree of certainty is that, at one point, the unexpected will come and kick you in the ass.

These few months were going to be busy regardless. In addition to writing this book, I'm deep into marketing my previous book, *The Obvious Choice*, keeping up with daily content on social media and operating my two companies.

By my count, that's four jobs. With Alison ill, I've added on caring for her, preparing meals, keeping the house tidy, and doing school pickups.

This wonderful, miraculous, incredible, indescribable moment in time when we anxiously await our third child, a child we'd both resigned to never having after so much heartbreak, could have otherwise been a terribly stressful affair.

On paper, the last month has been the busiest and most difficult of my life. And yet I feel at ease.

I have a friend who works a demanding job. So does his wife. Both make a lot of money, have a lot of professional responsibility.

They also have two kids. A few years older than ours. Both do extracurricular math tutoring and hockey many days a week. A full-time nanny helps around their house.

Their kids are orderly. They don't question their parents and they do as they're told. My boys, well, my oldest, Calvin, at least, is like me: disagreeable. Rules to him (and me) are considered suggestions. He doesn't fall into line just because some authority said that it's how things *are done here*.

Alison asked me my opinion on the difference between how we, versus our friends, are raising our kids. I don't know which is better: enforcing rules with an iron first so that kids obey or empowering children to talk back, find their way, screw up, break the rules, frustrate their parents, toe the line, and figure it out for themselves in a world where very little is black and white. I really don't.

What I said to Alison was that our friends don't have a choice. Their cups are full. No room for anything unexpected. Of course their kids have to obey the rules and rituals of the household. There is no other way that their household can operate. No space. Which is fine, until it isn't.

"You never know what you need until you need it. By then it's very often too late," I said to her.

Admittedly, we have an ideal situation for navigating Alison's illness.

Our family support is amazing. My parents live around the corner. Mom comes over almost every day to help with the kids.

We love our neighbors. Last night, for example, Calvin and Jaden had dinner at one of their houses while I cleaned our place, helped Alison, and prepped for the week.

And my work is flexible.

Some would say we're lucky. And we are. But it's not just luck. Only seems like it.

The quality of your life is downstream of the decisions that you make. Decisions made long ago. Decisions made without fully knowing whether they'll pay off. How they'll pay off. And, if they do, to what degree. Decisions whose ramifications are possible to appreciate only in retrospect. Or, most often, attributed to luck and fortune.

Years back, I decided against moving to New York City to fast-track my career. Trading professional opportunities for professional flexibility.

Alison and I could live anywhere in the world. Hawaii; Thailand; Panama. Pick your paradise. Enjoy year-round warmth. Get richer in tax havens. You name it. Instead, we bought a home in a place with high taxes where it's cold half of the year. That just so happens to be a six-minute-and-forty-nine second walk from my parents.

We didn't enroll Calvin in math tutoring after school. Maybe he won't get into as good a college. But because he isn't overloaded with after-school extracurriculars, the little dude runs around the neighborhood knocking on doors, asking friends to play, becoming comfortable around their families.

I know I've had advantages. Choices that some people don't get to make.

Not everyone can pick where they live. Not everyone has the option of family nearby. Not everyone can trade career advancement for flexibility. But I've seen people with way less than me create space in their lives and people with way more suffocate themselves.

The specifics look different for everyone. The principle doesn't: leave room for the unexpected. Wherever possible, resist the urge to fill every moment, spend every dollar, use every ounce of energy. Or, as we say in the fitness game, always leave two reps in the hole because if you don't you're gonna snap your shit up.

We didn't expect Alison to get pregnant. Well, that's not quite true. We expected her to get pregnant. We didn't expect her to *stay* pregnant. And we definitely didn't expect her to get so sick.

We also didn't expect one of our dearest friends, a close neighbor, to get diagnosed with an aggressive form of breast cancer two weeks ago. A house cleaner with two young daughters and no benefits who can't work for the foreseeable future.

It's Monday the twenty-eighth now, Eliane's first chemotherapy session. For two days after each treatment, she'll be sweating out the chemicals and shouldn't be around her kids. We love our friend's kids. They might sleep over at our house tonight. We don't know yet. I'll pick them up from school, and they'll have dinner at our place either way.

Real life happens. You can prepare yourself to go along for the ride. Or you can get hit by the car as it passes by. Building resilience is about getting strong when times are good so you can stand tall when they're not.

Don't fill your cup. Not because you can't. But because there's going to be something that will happen to you. Or to somebody you love. And when it does, you're going to be happy that you've left space.

"How to Build Resiliency to Manage Hardship," the article titles read. They promote reactive care solutions like yoga, guided meditation, and prayer. All useful things. But there's too much emphasis on reaction, not enough on prevention and preparedness.

People talk about work-life balance. I've never liked that. Balance is binary. Too precarious. If you're in balance, it means that you can also be in imbalance. I prefer the term *work-life harmony*. A flowing state where you roll with the punches.

Expect the unexpected. Build tolerance to life's intolerances. The best way to deal with something unhealthy is to first become as healthy as possible. Make decisions today that your future self will thank you for when shit hits the fan. Because it will.

THE HALF-FULL CUP

It's likely that you'll notice others who have decided to fill their cups to the brim get more attention, make more money, or even have better-behaved children. You might question your life's decisions to leave your cup half empty.

Until one day your wife gets pregnant and becomes bedridden. And then your neighbor gets cancer. And you're somehow not stressed and miserable. Instead, challenged. Grateful that you're able to enjoy the miracle of a pregnancy you never thought would happen. Grateful to be able to help a friend in need.

5.

The Paradox of Abundance

What you pursue has the power to either free you or quietly imprison you.

Marathons used to be twenty-five miles long. For the London Olympics in 1908, Queen Alexandra asked that the race start on Windsor Castle's lawn and end at the Olympic Stadium, a distance of 26.2 miles.

That's it.

That's why a modern marathon is 26.2 miles long and not 25.0.

The end of any race is nothing but a temporary marker without much significance.

This chapter isn't about eschewing achievement. Instead, it's about controlling your ambition, your ego, and your desire. Being excited for the future, without missing the magic in the present.

This chapter is about fitting the Tetris blocks of your life in the right order before it's too late.

Calvin begs me to read "just one more chapter" (three times a night) of his book. We're lying in his bed. My arm's around him. I'm tired. It's 9:30 p.m., and I'm working out at 7:00 a.m. tomorrow. I'm feeling behind on a book proposal and planned to sneak in some work on it.

I'm justifying to myself why I should say no to him.

Unhinged Habits

That I should kiss him good night, tell him that I love him, and leave his room.

That I need to go downstairs, uncap my pen, open my notebook, and get to work—*just this once*.

The price of making an exception to your values "just this once" often seems alluringly low. "It sucks you in," according to the Harvard professor Clayton Christensen, "and you don't see where that path is ultimately headed or the full cost that the choice entails." Left unchecked, "just this once" becomes cultural—embedded—hard to change. "Break one of my rules once, and I'm bound to break many more," wrote the author Haruki Murakami. It's a slippery slope.

My ninth grade math teacher put a sign above the clock in the classroom that read: "Clock watchers. Time will pass. You, however, may not."

There's a custom clock in my office. A beautiful wooden thing made from a fallen tree. On it, I asked the local artisan to burn three words: "Time passes, regardless." An homage to Ms. Choi's sign; a morbid reminder that your life is nothing more than one long string of special, yet expiring, moments, which will pass, regardless.

I'm still lying there with Calvin. My brain shifts into a less stupid gear.

Why am I in a rush to finish the proposal? I'm thinking. *Why am I in a rush to become somebody that I don't even like?*

The guilt I'm feeling for not working is because I have a kid. But my kid is literally the reason why I work.

The challenge we all face is one of immediacy. Our careers provide the clearest and most immediate evidence of achievement. Success stemming from investing time and energy into raising our kids or deepening the love with our spouse, on the other hand, cannot be measured for many years.

What follows are a few charts from the American Time Use Survey that break down who we spend our time with over the course of our lives. As you look at the following charts, I encourage you to reflect on how you invest your own time and whether you're happy with it.

The Paradox of Abundance

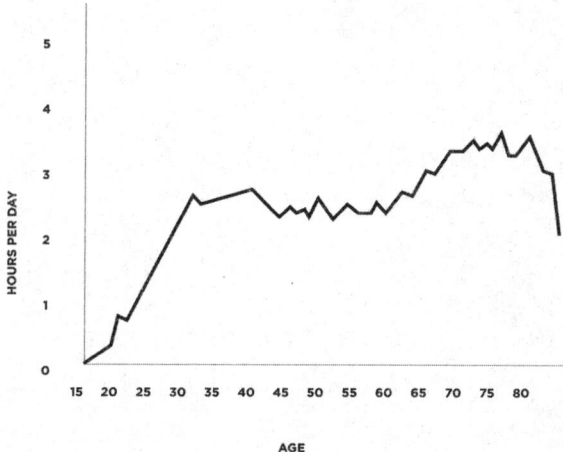

Time spent with coworkers peaks around age twenty and stays relatively consistent through our thirties, forties, and fifties before falling off. Work pulls you away from loved ones during what many consider their best years. If you have the luxury, question the forces that keep you at work and away from the people you love. Is it necessary? Is it worth it? Will you even remember the important work thing keeping you away from your family in a month, let alone ten years? (@Unhinged Habits)

Unhinged Habits

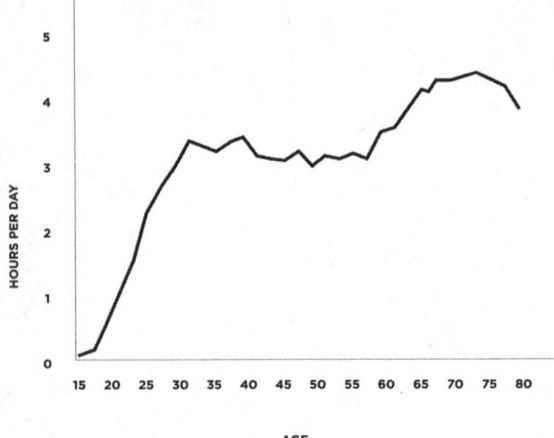

Time spent with your partner stays mostly flat throughout your years until your sixties, at which point it rises dramatically. Choosing your partner is the most important decision you will ever make. Ongoing investments into deepening the relationship with them during your busy middle years is the best thing you can do to improve the quality of life for your future self. (@Unhinged Habits)

The Paradox of Abundance

Time Spent With Children

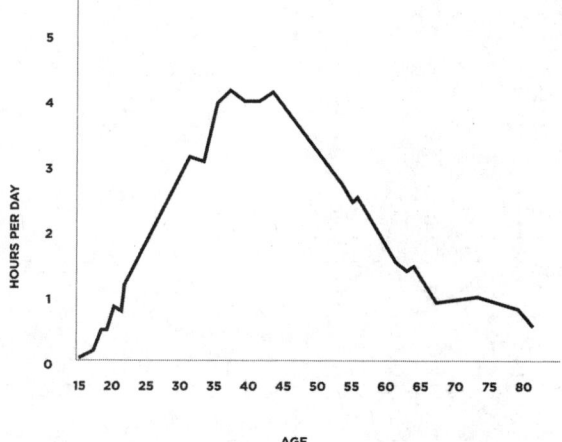

Time spent with children spikes for a few years in your thirties and early forties before falling off a cliff. It's a devastatingly short window. Blink and you'll miss it. Slow down. Play Monopoly. Read them books on repeat. The time you spend with your children is never wasted. (@Unhinged Habits)

Unhinged Habits

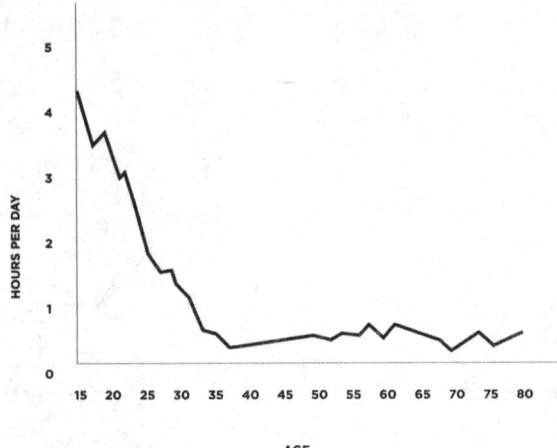

Time spent with family declines sharply after adolescence. Cherish moments with extended family, siblings, and, especially, parents. With our ambitions and the busyness of our days, it is far too easy to forget how limited the time we have left with them truly is. A phone call or quick trip to connect with parents if they live far away is always a good idea. (@Unhinged Habits)

Mark 8:36 in the Bible reads, "What shall it profit a man, if he shall gain the whole world, and lose his own soul?" Hurry, busyness, and ambition are double-edged swords. Money can buy a bed, but it can't buy a good night's sleep.

Being driven to success in life often results in living a mediocre version of it.

Workaholism is how you lose yourself, not find yourself. A crutch. Wrongly, it seems entirely justified at the time, at *any time*. Sadly, the only people who will remember that you worked late will be your kids.

The Paradox of Abundance

It's easy to fall into the trap of marginal thinking. Of justifying to yourself why you should make an exception "just this once." And perhaps if it really were just this once, then that wouldn't be a problem. But it never is, is it?

The real game of life is internal. There's no big bad boss. We're our only enemy. It's like *Tetris*, where getting a high score depends on a strong foundation. Good choices divide; bad choices multiply. According to the writer David Charles, who once spent a whole summer playing the game, "An early mistake is always lurking there to trip you up. You've got to dig down and sort it out sooner or later or you won't get anywhere. Sorting yourself out can take a long time, but it's always possible."

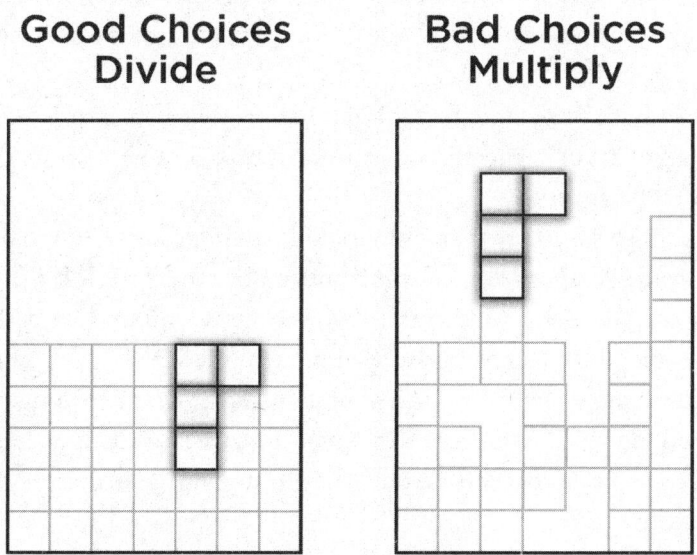

In the game of life, good choices divide and bad choices multiply. You can always end with a good outcome but the longer you wait, the bigger the mess you'll have to clean up becomes. (©Unhinged Habits)

The filmmaker Chris Higgins wrote that *Tetris* has three additional key features:

1. You cannot win, only play.

Unhinged Habits

2. You must accept what comes to you as it comes.
3. Everything goes faster and faster until it ends.

Good analogy.

The older you get, the busier you become. Everything immediate seems more important in the moment than it actually is.

Here's a hard take: time-saving devices don't save time.

Productivity apps, journals, and to-do lists don't shrink work; they expand expectations.

You'll never be on top of everything because everything constantly expands. There's no "when I finish this I'll have time to become the person I want to be." That's not how it works.

Once you successfully automate one job, delegate another, make a pile of money, or fix your to-do list, your conveyor belt speeds up, bringing you new things to do.

Not only that, but the better a reputation that you earn from quickly finishing your work, and the more you squeeze into your time, the more stuff you'll be given to do.

None of this is to say that you should knowingly do a bad job or reduce your output. Weaponizing your incompetence might work for things like folding the laundry badly so that your wife gives in and lets you hire a house cleaner, but it's a bad general approach to life.

Instead, you have to stop believing that the answer lies in figuring out how to do more. The counterintuitive way to have more is to do less, better. To make the hard decisions about what to do with your time and accept its trade-offs.

Oliver Burkeman, in his wonderful book *Four Thousand Weeks*, summed it up beautifully when he wrote: "Once you truly understand that you're guaranteed to miss out on almost every experience the world has to offer, the fact that there are so many you still haven't experienced stops feeling like a problem. Instead, you get to focus on fully enjoying the tiny slice of experiences you actually do have time for—and the freer you are to choose, in each moment, what counts the most."

He later added: "You have to choose a few things, sacrifice everything else, and deal with the inevitable sense of loss that results."

Amen.

The Paradox of Abundance

Calvin is seven years old. The days where we snuggle in bed reading stories together are numbered. And so the work that the dumb part of my brain feels I have to do tonight can wait. It's more important for me to lie in bed with him and read *Charlie and the Chocolate Factory* until I lose my voice and he falls asleep with his head on my chest while I still can. Because soon, this fleeting period will pass. And when that does, I'll have plenty of time to work on book proposals at night, sadly.

THE "WHEN I FINALLY" TRAP

A text message Trevor Kasey sent to a friend read, "Investment managers, despite pitches, make their money by skimming off the top NOW."

The notion that we can somehow compete for prizes, get them, quit the game, and live out the rest of our days joyously fulfilled is a gamble many make, often to the detriment of their present well-being.

The work you feel you have to do today just means something you'll laugh at in five years. Value the stuff you won't laugh at. Like love. Or a good book. Or your health.

Like the 26.2 mile distance in a marathon, somebody made up rules. (Maybe that somebody was you and those rules only exist in your mind.) Regardless, those rules, like any path, self-reinforce over time.

If you're not careful, the endless search for status will lead you into the trap of insecure overachievement. Seeking to win whatever the game is, only to get to the end and realize that you haven't been playing the game, the game has been playing you. That you shouldn't have been playing by the rules; you should have been making your own.

"People were always getting ready for tomorrow," wrote Cormac McCarthy. "I didn't believe in that. Tomorrow wasn't getting ready for them. It didn't even know they were there." This future-focused approach can best be described as the "when-I-finally" trap.

"When I finally have more money I'll become philanthropic," we say, with the best of intentions. "When my kids finally go to school I'll get into shape," we ambitiously tell our family. "When I finally finish this work project I'll host a dinner party," we think.

Unhinged Habits

It's easy to assume that getting rich in money will also mean that you're rich in time. More commonly, it's the opposite. Earning more money results in less time and more responsibilities. The same goes with success.

"I'll be happy when _____." Fill in the blank. It could be anything. If you're secretly saying this, whatever you put in that blank space will keep changing.

This future-focused postponement is so common that we often don't recognize it in ourselves.

Take a moment to consider a few common when-I-finally traps. Once done, feel free to write in any of your own meaningful experiences or actions that you're currently delaying until some arbitrary future condition is met. I've left you three blank spaces.

A few common "when-I-finally" traps

What I'm waiting for	What I'm postponing	How long I've been waiting
When we finish renovating the house	Invite friends for dinner regularly	1.5 years
When I get promoted	Spend more time with kids	2 years
When I'm not so busy at work	Call my parents more regularly	2.5 years
When I lose 20 pounds	Join a rec sports league	3 years
When I have more money saved	Take that trip to Japan	4 years
When the kids are older	Rekindle my relationship with my spouse	5 years

A useful question to ask: Are you delaying meaningful experiences until you meet arbitrary future conditions that are prone to shift beyond your reach? (©Unhinged Habits)

Yes, you should consider your future. But not at the detriment of your present.

The artist formerly known as Prince once held a party after he performed on *Saturday Night Live*. There was a DJ and a little buffet with macaroni and cheese. Because of course there was.

The comedian Fred Armisen walked up to him and said, "I just wanted to tell you. I think that you are the greatest."

Prince was sitting by himself. He looked up.

"You know what I think the greatest is?" Prince asked.

"What's that?"

"This macaroni and cheese."

No matter how much success we have. Or how high we climb. We're all going to find ourselves eating mac and cheese on the couch. So, maybe, we should enjoy it.

There's no nirvana to look forward to in your later years if you pinch pennies and forgo joy today. One huge event won't bring happiness. Instead, it's the many small things day to day that will bring a smile to your face. Like talking to your mailman. Or a bike ride with a friend. Or the feeling of juice dripping down your chin from a freshly picked Honeycrisp apple in the fall.

A valuable reframe: if your job gives you the freedom to have coffee with your partner, lunch with friends, dinner with your family, and exercise regularly, you're already successful.

PRICE VERSUS DIGNITY

Value exists in two forms: as means to something else or as an end in itself.

Means are stepping stones to get somewhere else. Money becomes valuable only once it's exchanged. Nobody goes to a personal trainer because they love Bulgarian split squats (nobody loves Bulgarian split squats). They go because they want the results. Making money and lifting weights are both worth doing, but they're not the end game.

Ends are different. They're worth doing for their own sake. Playing with your child. Sunday morning snuggles with your wife. The satisfaction of creating art with your own two hands. These experiences need no justification beyond themselves.

We all begin with dreams centered on final values: "I'm going to live a healthy life." "One day I'll write a book." "I want to sing in a band." But then reality hits. Bills pile up. Expenses increase. Jobs and lifestyles lock us in, pushing those dreams further away, sometimes forever.

Immanuel Kant framed this distinction perfectly: there's price and then there's dignity. Anything with price can be replaced. It's a means, not the end. Dignity stands above price. It's the end, not the means. Over time, wisdom lies in exchanging more things with price for things with dignity.

The longer you spend chasing things with price while postponing things with dignity, the harder it becomes to escape the trap. Every decision you make becomes evidence of who you are, creating a self-reinforcing loop through your identity, network, and habits.

Samantha built a career in talent agency work that perfectly matched her organizational skills and network-building abilities. Throughout her twenties and early thirties, she worked relentlessly—long hours, constant travel, and the industry's standard late dinners and drinks.

She thrived, eventually running her agency's entire Canadian operation. Success bred more opportunity, and when an international leadership role opened, everyone expected her to jump at it.

She didn't.

"It would have meant more money, bigger clients, and definitely more industry recognition," she told me over a game of pool. "But I asked myself what I'd be trading for those things."

The answer was clear: more flights, more late nights, more weekends away from her husband and kids, and even less time for the health habits she was working to rebuild.

"Ten years ago, I would have taken it without thinking twice," she said. "But I've realized something important: ambition isn't wrong, but chaotic ambition without boundaries is a fire that burns your life to ash while you stand there holding the match.

"At first, people were surprised when I didn't apply," she continued. "But now people praise me for having the control to recognize when, for me, enough was enough." Samantha didn't abandon her career. She still runs the Canadian division. She simply recognized when the price of the next rung on the ladder exceeded its dignity.

With each choice, you're either moving toward a life of dignity or one dictated by price tags. Here's what this looks like in practice:

What we chase versus what we're really after

Means (Price)	Ends (Dignity)
Home theater system	Quality time with family
Travel	Meaningful and formative experiences
Designer clothing	Personal style / self-expression
Buying a new bike	Weekend rides with friends or family
Expensive coffee from an indie café	Supporting local community
Hiring a personal trainer	Being physically healthy / improved perception of sexification
High-end journal or productivity planner	Clarity of purpose and intention
Meditation app subscription	Inner peace and emotional regulation
Standing desk / walking pad	Energy and vitality throughout the workday

Consider what you're actually seeking with your purchases when considering both the tangible item you acquire and the deeper experience you truly desire. The gap between the two reveals whether your money buys short-term satiation or genuine fulfillment. (©Unhinged Habits)

EXTRA BRAIN SPACE

Money and success aren't change catalysts; they're amplification agents.

If you're adventurous, money will help you go on more and greater adventures. But if you're not, it won't.

If you're a good person. A moral person. A generous person, caring, loving, and well-adjusted, money and success will amplify all that's good. But it doesn't pick and choose. If you're a selfish person. A person driven by greed, absorbed by envy, unhappy, lonely, and overworked, then no amount of money will change you. There's no "when I finally," and things will be better. If you live a life poor in values, more money will make matters worse. You can't poison the well and then complain about the water.

Andrew Carnegie died in 1919 as one of the richest men in the world. Here's a small list of things we take for granted that he couldn't have because they weren't invented yet: central heating, penicillin, commercial air travel, and television.

These days, your haves are greater than the have nots.

Just about anything that measurably improves a level-headed person's quality of life—laundry machines, cars that drive the speed limit, the internet—are democratized, available to all. The truth? Poverty is really hard, and middle-class life is a real gift, but after that it's the law of diminishing returns.

So long as you have a relatively low baseline of wealth, you can afford luxuries that even the richest people in the world didn't dream of a hundred years ago.

The truth about acquisition is that you quickly normalize to your new possessions. We spoke about this before. It's called hedonic adaptation. Do you remember? It's the tendency to return to a baseline level of happiness regardless of positive changes in your circumstances.

The new phone you waited in line for? After a month, it's just your phone.

That kitchen renovation you spent a year planning? By summer, it's just your kitchen again.

My buddy Jason saved for five years to buy his dream car. A Tesla. It cost him $75,000. For the first few weeks, he'd find excuses to drive anybody, anywhere. By the second month, it was just his car that took him from A to B.

Jenny's somebody I know here in Mexico. She was a corporate bigwig with a huge wardrobe back in the States. Each morning, she'd stress over what to wear. One day, she decided enough was enough and donated half of her clothes to charity.

"It's like my brain has extra space now." Jenny told me that she didn't realize how much her abundance was causing exhausting decisions that were draining her every day.

The Paradox of Abundance

Owning too many things doesn't enhance our lives; it paralyzes and exhausts us. Abundance, therefore, is a paradox.

Ever stared at the Netflix menu for twenty minutes only to give up and go to bed? Me too. That's decision fatigue.

Ever spent an hour researching the perfect restaurant for dinner only to enjoy it less because you're second-guessing whether the other place might have been better? Me too. That's the dark side of too many options.

There aren't many things of consequence available only to the rich anymore. Private air travel is one. That's all that I can think of. But the same ice-cold minican of Coke Zero at 2:00 p.m., the most glorious of drinks at the most glorious of times, sits in my fridge and a billionaire's fridge. Maybe a billionaire has a nicer fridge. But mine keeps my drinks cold just fine. What I love about life right now is that no matter how much money Bezos has, he can't get a better Coke Zero than me. And he probably has less time to enjoy it too.

At a certain point, "wealth is like sea water," said Arthur Schopenhauer. "The more we drink, the thirstier we become; and the same is true of fame."

Stop the endless search for the pot of joy at the end of the hedonistic rainbow.

EGO AND QUIMIXTO

I admitted to Alison something I dislike about myself, which is that I feel like I deserve more public recognition for the way I live my life.

"Yeah, but you don't actually want that," she said.

I didn't understand what she meant, so I did that thing where I paused so she'd continue.

"If you had more public admiration for your life's choices, it would unconsciously impact those choices. Which would make your life worse."

She's right.

Too many leaders today start off as servants but end up as celebrities. They then become addicted to attention, unaware of how the spotlight is changing them. "If there were such a thing as sin, this would be it: to allow yourself to become what you are because of the experience of others," wrote Neale Donald Walsch in *Conversations with God*.

Unhinged Habits

Like domesticated oxen, these people become driven by what their audience perceives of them. Higher engagement will always result from sensationalistic content, divisive opinions, or extreme, fake, and unrealistic lifestyles. In many cases, a person has a loose opinion that gets a strong response, which reinforces their opinion, leading to them stating it more often and more forcefully, becoming changed in the process.

When we had that conversation, Alison and I were enjoying two nights away at a beachside cabaña in a remote area of Mexico called Quimixto. Despite it being lifestyle-influencer heaven, neither of us took a picture. We were there, together, for us to live and love and connect away from the kids. The thought of how I might be able to craft the experience into content never crossed my mind.

Nobody should ever be there but not be present with family because they're thinking about something clever to say on social media about what they're doing.

Your motivation must not be to get rich or famous but to be seen as significant in the eyes of the few people who love you. "The only true test of intelligence is if you get what you want out of life," according to Naval Ravikant. I later heard him say that there are two parts to the intelligence test:

1. Are you able to hack reality to get what you want?
2. Are you smart enough to figure out what you want in the first place?

I've got a friend with millions of followers. His social media is an all-encompassing obsession. He can't stop growing it. His ego doesn't allow a pause. It leads his life. His friends are friends he collabs with. He travels with a bulky camera. And he often pulls out his phone when he's with his wife and kids to write down an idea he just had for a post. My friend lives his life being there but not present.

I don't know whether he's happy doing what he's doing, but we do talk often. He's said some variation of "when my accounts finally get to a certain size, I'll start my book" more than once.

There's a critical difference between using social media and being used by it. One is strategic and bounded; the other is consuming and identity forming. The distinction isn't about whether you use these platforms but how and why you use them.

"It's been over three years. You haven't started yet," I said to him one day.

No response. So I continued.

"You've got millions of followers. How big do your accounts need to get?"

This guy designed his life around social media. His friends are all friends with benefits of a different kind, the kind who support one another to grow online.

Is he ever going to flip a switch, change his way of being, and fully commit to the grind of book writing without the instant gratification that comes with the daily dopamine provided by likes and shares?

I doubt it.

Notoriety and recognition are fine if viewed as fortunate byproducts of doing the right work, the right way. When they're stated as the goal; when building a following is the goal; when making money when you already have enough is the goal; when anything other than the love for your work and the love for the people you surround yourself with is the goal, you'll be led down a path whose destination can be described only as *unhappy*.

Society tells you to have good values but rewards you for turning your back on them. This is nothing new. Rollo May wrote about the contradiction in his book *Psychology and the Human Dilemma* way back in 1967: "You are said to be significant, but it is a significance that is brought precisely at the price of giving up your significance."

Time to check in with myself . . .

I'm jealous of my friend. I'm jealous of the attention that he gets. A part of me that I don't like feels like I deserve what he has. Which is dumb. He's worked hard for it. I've worked hard for other things. But that's how I feel.

Being jealous of what somebody has is different from being jealous of how they got it. It's okay to admire others without desiring the life that they've had to live in order to have it. Next time you're jealous of somebody, think, *Are you jealous of them as a whole or just a piece of them you wish that you had? Would you trade your life for theirs? All of it?*

Unhinged Habits

Whenever I find myself in a comparison funk to this guy, I run a cost-benefit analysis and quickly decide that, as good as his numbers look on my screen, I wouldn't trade places. I want his following. I'm jealous of his following. But his life would make me miserable. I'm not willing to do what he does. I don't want to be thinking of something witty or wise when I'm in a beachside cabaña with my wife. I don't want to wait for the perfect lighting to take a photo. I'd rather leave my phone at home and skinny dip and eat cold watermelon and lose track of time.

So far, my friend has committed three years to his online following. During those same three years, I've written one and a half books. That's right for him. And what I do is right for me.

Nobody talks about the in-between times enough, only what's next.

Sometimes there isn't a "what's next" yet though. Sometimes we're in between. In those times, the best things to focus on are skill development, networking, or, as was my case in 2021, improving my options by growing an online platform.

For a year and a half, I didn't know what my next move was. At first, it was a source of stress. Then I leaned into the in-between and decided to grow my social media accounts.

I felt the tension. *"Wasn't this the same trap I criticized others for falling into?"* I asked myself.

Not quite.

The difference was in my relationship to social media: I approached it as a tool with boundaries, not as an identity or primary focus. Whatever did come next, whenever I figured it out, would benefit from a larger launchpad. It wasn't quite a full-time job, but it absorbed a lot of my best creative energy.

My advice to entrepreneurs: build your online platform whenever you're not deep in a project.

Near the end of the year, I started feeling a pull to write another book. I'd told myself that I wasn't going to write another book until I couldn't *not* write another book. That time had come. I felt the fire. That book turned into *The Obvious Choice*. This one's followed.

The Paradox of Abundance

What's next, for me, has become full-fledged authorship. An all-consuming endeavor. The trade-off for my "next" was that growing my social media got relegated to the back seat. Appropriately viewed as a byproduct of success in other areas. A lagging indicator of great work, not leading. By then, my following was big enough. Not huge by any influencer's measure but enough of a launchpad that if my books are great, they'd be given the chance that they need to succeed given a long-enough time horizon.

A big social media platform won't make a bad product successful; it'll make it fail faster. If a thing sucks, it sucks. No audience can save that. On the flip side, a great product with no distribution network might never get the initial critical mass of people it needs in order to have the chance it deserves.

The key isn't whether you have a social media following—it's your relationship to it. Does it serve your deeper work, or does your work serve it? Is it a means or is it an end? For my friend, followers became the end. For me, I'm trying to ensure it stays a means.

Competition, not personal betterment, leads to a misguided desire to acquire. Envy's the enemy of contentment. Your ego wants more than you want to have. The truth is that we only envy the people closest to us. Family members envy one another. Neighbors envy neighbors. And colleagues envy colleagues.

I guess if you want to be really happy and you're middle class, the best way to do it would be to move into a poor neighborhood. Then you'll have nobody to envy. Unless you log on to the internet. Yeah, that wouldn't even work.

Objectively, it's irrelevant who's better off. Like, if I'm doing well and so is that other guy, isn't that a good thing?

Only secure people thrive.

Insecure people become absorbed with how they appear to others for reasons they cannot explain.

"A man who does big things is too busy to talk about them," reads a passage from *Letters from a Self-Made Merchant*. "When the jaws really need exercise, chew gum."

The flashier the Instagram profile, the more perfectly manicured the social media, and the more confident the online exterior, the more likely it is that the entire thing is a charade. That the owner of that account is overcompensating for their confusion, anxiety, and lack of purpose. Like a dude popping bottles at the club, they're seeking significance through prominence in the wrong place.

GOOD MEMORIES

Jason texted me. He was in Costa Rica with his family; their first-ever vacation.

"How's it going?" I asked.

"Chaos, lol!" he responded. The kids were giving him a hard time.

That's no fun. Right? You go on an adventure with your family, and it's exhausting and stressful. The kids aren't listening even though you're doing it for them, and don't they understand, don't they get, that you spent so much money and took time off work for them, and why don't they even appreciate it . . .

This experience makes no sense, we think. *God get me out of this,* we pray. But it's often when we get out of it that we understand why God put us in it.

Despite everything going on, Jason's with his family in the jungle seeing monkeys. MONKEYS.

Okay, so I've been in a lot of jungles with monkeys, and truthfully most monkeys are a pain in the ass. One time my wife and I were in Manuel Antonio in Costa Rica; we were lying in bed, and three different kinds of monkeys were climbing on our balcony. We couldn't go outside because it was dangerous. The monkeys were stealing our food. They figured out how to open cupboards, and they shit everywhere, and it was a whole thing. But also, MONKEYS.

Doing something—even if everything goes wrong—even if monkeys steal your food and shit everywhere or your kids are brats (and steal your food and shit everywhere)—results in good memories. Sometimes, the worse the experience, the better the memories. Reminiscing about how bad something was is actually really fun. And because you get to do it long

The Paradox of Abundance

after the actual experience, it paradoxically brings more long-term joy than a positive experience would have brought.

You never get to replay a decision. It's like, the bus is coming: You can run to catch it or wait for the next.

Each bus has different people and timetables. Odds are, in the case of catching two buses a few minutes apart, you won't notice the impact of one choice over another. But think about it. How many different things can happen? And how many little choices do we make each day with divergent paths?

It's a hard concept for me to even wrap my head around.

You'll only ever get to find out what's behind door number one. Even if the result is positive, you'll always wonder, "What if. . . . ?"

Regrets are unavoidable. Make yours regrets of commission, not omission. Of the things you did, not that you didn't do.

If something doesn't work out the way that you planned, it's more likely to work out in a way that you never could have anticipated than if you didn't do anything. Paul Millerd calls this the Pathless Path. I like that.

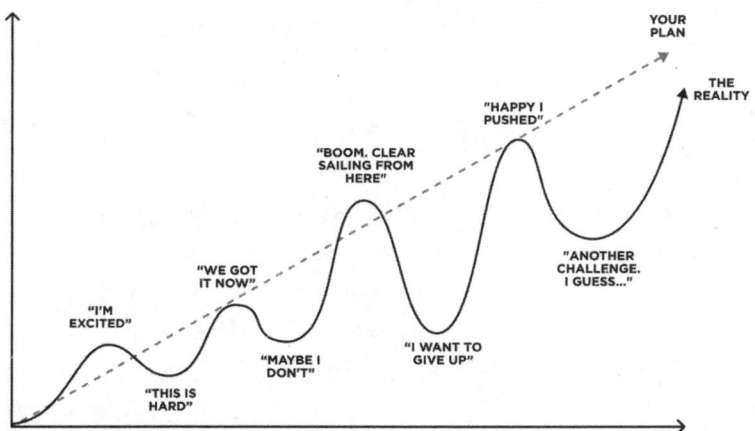

It is virtually guaranteed that things will not work out precisely according to your plan, but the odds are good that things will work out in a way you could have never anticipated before you began. The secret, therefore, is to start, fully embracing the inevitable unpredictability that will follow. (©Unhinged Habits)

Unhinged Habits

Life has a way of going well for people who do stuff and not going well for people who sit at home and plot and plan and make excuses for not doing stuff *yet*.

Even if it goes awry, you'll learn something if you do something. That's fluffy self-help, but it's true. Thoreau's got this line I can't get out of my head: "Oh God, to reach the point of death only to find that you have never lived at all."

If you ever go back and do a full accounting of your life—which you won't, but if you did—you'd find that most everything good that happened to you was the result of random things you learned and random experiences that you had that got mashed together in a way impossible to explain or reproduce. Call it the human experience or whatever. It doesn't matter. All that I know is that this is what separates us from computers and what brings color to our existence.

In 1949, there was a national Gallup Poll that asked adults to identify the biggest mistake of their life so far. Just a few years later, in 1953, a similar poll was conducted with a variation on the question. It asked, "If you could live your life over again, would you live it in much the same way as you have, or would you live it differently?"

The first question identifies mistakes, the second regrets. In response to the first question, more than 69 percent were willing to admit a mistake. Less than 40 percent, on the other hand, said that they'd live differently if they could do it again.

Think about a recent mistake that you made. Got it. Okay, now, because it happened in the past, you can consider the impact that it's had on you.

Surely it challenged you. Strengthened your resolve. Taught you a thing or two about yourself, about others, and about how your world works. Maybe it changed your path, setting you down the road you're on now.

Do you actually regret your mistake? Or, with the benefit of hindsight, are you oddly grateful for that terrible thing that happened because of what it taught you, how it strengthened you, and what it led to? You needn't have wished for something to happen in order to be grateful that it did.

The Paradox of Abundance

We all start in the same race, running toward arbitrary goals. Degrees. Promotions. Acquisitions. Followers. Higher income. Bigger houses. Better cars.

But like that 26.2-mile marathon distance created for a queen's viewing pleasure, most finish lines in our lives are completely made up. Temporary markers without much significance.

The time charts don't lie. The window with your children closes faster than you imagine. The years with your parents are numbered. Your spouse becomes your primary companion in later years, but only if you've nurtured that relationship along the way.

Your values define the race you're running, not your possessions. The means serve a purpose, but the ends are what give life its meaning.

One day, Barrett and Katy were walking together in the Crown Hill Nature Reserve in Denver. The Powerball lottery was up over a billion dollars. "What would we do if we won this? Where would we live?" Barrett asked.

Well, they decided, they'd have a place in New York City and a ski chalet in Breckenridge. And then they'd live in Lawrence, Kansas—the town they grew up in—where their friends still live.

Then Barrett looked at Katy and said, "What are we doing living in Denver?" Within a year they had moved back to Lawrence.

I have a party trick. Three questions I love to ask.

If you had unlimited amounts of money—Bezos level wealth—how would you live your life differently?

What would you start doing?

What would you keep doing?

What would you stop doing?

I like these questions because they shine a spotlight on the good.

People tend to discover that whatever they desire, if forced to dream as big as they can possibly dream, is actually within their grasp today. It's their own fear stopping them. Or they're being distracted by meaningless frivolities. Both wonderful revelations.

When you know you have enough, you become fearless. Free to explore things that interest you; free to ignore those that don't serve you; and most of all, free to fail. With enough, you can make mistakes. Which is awesome. Because even bad mistakes make for good memories.

Next, let's categorize your friends.

CHAPTER 5 SUMMARY

- **Recognize who you're spending your limited time with.** Your career provides immediate (and addictive) evidence of achievement, but the time with children, partners, and parents operates on a much shorter (and expiring) timeline than most realize.

- **Maintain a healthy relationship with success and recognition.** When notoriety becomes the goal rather than a byproduct of meaningful work, it distorts your priorities and decisions, ultimately changing who you are.

- **Choose dignity over price.** Pursue experiences with inherent worth (dignity) rather than those that merely serve as means to other ends (price). The longer you chase things with price while postponing things with dignity, the harder it becomes to escape.

- **Escape the "when-I-finally" trap.** Stop postponing meaningful experiences and relationships until arbitrary future conditions are met. The endless cycle of deferred living never reaches a natural conclusion.

6.

The Joy of Fewer Friends

Prioritize social depth over breadth.

Eighty-five years of research from Harvard University concluded that your relationships are the single greatest predictor of your happiness. Not money. Not career achievement. Not the number of countries you've visited or the size of your home.

But in a world obsessed with productivity, followers, and networking, we've forgotten something essential: the depth of our connections matters more than their breadth.

This chapter isn't about having more friends. It's about maintaining a healthy ecosystem of community connections while having the courage to invest your limited time and energy selectively. It's about designing your social life with intentionality.

Is ruthlessly auditing your social life callous? Maybe. Is it necessary? Absolutely.

Day three of a coastal ATV trip in Costa Rica. Alison and I stumble upon a hotel. We're covered in dirt. They have a shower. We stop.

After a meal, we say thank you to the waiter.

"Goodbye. Have a nice life," he replied.

I love that.

Unhinged Habits

An admission that he was never going to see us again. That we shared time together. That it was nice. And that it is over.

I'm writing this to you from Mexico. It's November. We're here until April.

There's a family we had dinner with last night. We like them. Our kids get along. They leave tomorrow. Going home. Somewhere in the Midwestern USA. Kansas, I think. Maybe they'll be back in March. If so, we'll be happy to see them again. But we won't keep in touch in between.

People come and go. Living their life. Passing through yours.

Don't feel guilty for letting loose friendships lapse. It's perfectly okay to enjoy a fleeting moment with another while simultaneously appreciating that almost every relationship you have had (and will ever have) is short-lived.

That, in the words of Brian A. Chalker, "people come into your life for a reason, a season, or a lifetime and, when you figure out which one it is, you will know what to do for each person."

Sure, exchange phone numbers or emails if that makes you feel good. You'll never use either. Which is fine.

When it comes to adult friendship, it's helpful to categorize your relationships using a garden metaphor so that you can understand how different connections serve different purposes.

THE GARDEN OF FRIENDSHIP

Think of your social life as a garden that you cultivate with grass, flowers, birds, and tree(s). Like any good garden, it contains different types of plants and visitors, each playing a unique role in the ecosystem.

First, the *grass*—your professional networks, colleagues, or people whose relationship with you is primarily based on what you can do for one another. "Deal friends" I've also heard them referred to.

These people serve a practical purpose. They're spread across the ground of your social landscape, not always distinctly noticeable but helpful in providing basic coverage and support despite their shallow roots.

Grass connections need regular upkeep. If the usefulness of one person to another were to end, so does the friendship. When the season changes or new growth emerges, these connections may die off, be trimmed back, or get replaced. Which is fine.

Next up, you have the *flowers*—people you enjoy sharing activities with, live close to, or with whom your paths currently overlap.

These are your neighbors, pickleball buddies, church friends, or that nice family you see every year on vacation who you think lives in Kansas and whose names you can't remember but it's become awkward to ask so you say buddy to the dad, and that's fine; but you are still searching for a similar way to greet the mom.

Call them acquaintances. Flowers are welcome colorful additions to your garden that bring you joy when they are in season, making your social life more vibrant.

Some are perennial and return as predictably as summer's bloom, cycling through your life in rhythmic patterns. Picture the parents you meet at your daughter's weekly gymnastics practice or the classmates you had each school year. These are friends whose paths intersect with yours repeatedly for more than one cyclical season.

Others are annuals, existing for a single, ephemeral season, never to return again. Think the friendly travelers you meet on a specific trip or members of the team that you work with on a volunteer project in your city. These connections bloom brilliantly but briefly, leaving behind a snapshot of a moment in time, vibrant yet transient.

Next in your garden are the *birds*—their presence enhances your garden without requiring care or attention. You recognize them, but they don't know you exist.

These are the content creators, celebrities, and public figures whose lives you follow from afar. You can enjoy them in comfort from a distance either by yourself or with others who happen to share your interests.

And finally, the *tree(s)*—your true friend(s).

These are sturdy and enduring friends that weather all seasons. They provide shade in summer, shelter in storms, and remain steadfast through winters. Their growth is slow but meaningful, and they become more special and meaningful with time.

Put it all together, and you've got your Garden of Friendship:

Grass—Professional connections that provide basic coverage and practical support

Flowers—Seasonal acquaintances who bring joy when your paths naturally cross

Birds—One-sided relationships with people you watch but who don't know you exist

Tree(s)—True friends who remain steadfast across all seasons

THE GARDEN OF FRIENDSHIP

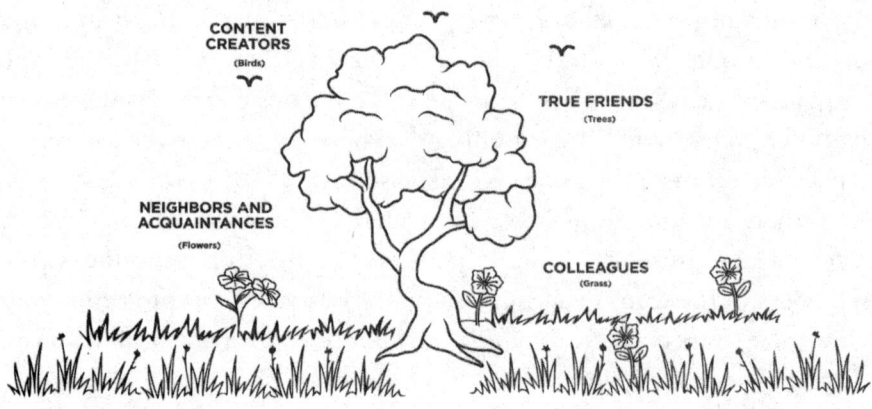

Think of your friendship ecosystem as a garden where professional connections (grass) provide the foundation, acquaintances (flowers) add seasonal color, content creators (birds) enrich from afar, and true friends (trees) offer enduring support and shelter. (©Unhinged Habits)

MY ONE FRIEND

I have one friend. His name is Andrew.

Andrew likes stability; I need chaos. He likes vacations; I crave adventure. He works a normal job; I've given up trying to figure out what I'm going to do when I grow up.

Despite our differences, you could lock us in a room for a month, and when you open the door, we'll be talking and laughing. About what? I'm not sure.

If he needs help, I'm there.
Is pissed off and wants to vent, I'll listen.
Has something to celebrate, I'm bro-hugging him.
And vice versa, of course.

When our schedules become overloaded, we start skimming relationally. "Busyness is the great enemy of relationships," wrote the pastor John Mark Comer. Social incentives push us toward deal friends and away from real friends.

If you've got a hangout with a friend and something comes up at work, you'll cancel on your friend and say, "I've got a thing." But we don't do the opposite. We don't approach friendship with the same intentionality.

Imagine sending an email to your boss saying, "Hey, Mr. Thomas Taylor. First off, love how your name alliterates. Not sure if I've told you that before. Also, hate to do this, but need to reschedule our performance eval. I've got a thing. My friend asked me to hang. Miss him. We're probably just gonna smash some tacos; shoot the shit. Felt it was more important."

Many of us will see our friends only if we don't have work. Everyone in your life knows this. They'll even admit it. "If you're not working, can you . . . ," they'll say.

Deal friends—the grass—will naturally show up over the course of your career. These are friends you maintain because you need or want something. You don't necessarily use this person. The benefits might be mutual. But they'll come and go. And, secretly, though rarely stated outright, both people know the deal.

None of this means that you don't generally like the person or enjoy their company. But if you were to remove the potential for career advancement, greater social access, or whatever other goal that you feel they help you achieve, the friendship would dissolve.

In a busy life you can't realistically maintain too many true friendships—just a couple or, in my case, just one. To that person, the highest compliment you can pay them is "you are useless to me." Perfect friendship must exist outside of your job and ambition.

Unhinged Habits

The paradox of friendship is that our deepest need is for people we don't need at all. Uselessness, therefore, is the first of the three proxies of true friendship. The best friends can do nothing for you.

We have a giant oak tree on my property. Having a big tree was the single nonnegotiable I had when buying a home. It can't be bought or cheated. Trees take time to grow.

Oh, how I love that tree. My office pod was designed to have a large window facing it. My parents read to my kids under its canopy. Sometimes, when no one's looking, I touch its bark to feel its energy.

But this magnificent tree comes with trade-offs. Its sprawling canopy blocks sunlight for much of our yard. Its vast root system depletes the soil of nutrients and water. Grass struggles to grow beneath it, and planting anything else nearby is futile.

Having a giant tree is a trade-off. Which makes it the perfect metaphor for true friendship. A true friend demands the time, energy, and attention that might otherwise nurture many other smaller connections. Having one means accepting that some parts of your social garden will remain in shadow. But like my oak tree, the shelter, stability, and beauty it provides make the sacrifice worthwhile.

Of course, relationships can shift.

My mother-in-law's closest friends today are people she worked with for decades. Throughout their careers, they maintained collegial relationships. Deal friends, useful to one another professionally. Their relationship transformed after retirement, when the utility of work that bound them was removed.

Major life transitions often catalyze these shifts, revealing which work relationships were always rooted in something deeper than mere utility.

We live close to the airport. My in-laws are thirty minutes in the opposite direction.

One night, after a long day with the kids, my wife picked her mom up after a flight, drove her home, and then drove back home. It was a two-hour round trip. Her mom could have easily taken a cab. I offered to pay for a car service.

The Joy of Fewer Friends

"Acts of service are how we show love for one another," Alison said.

I have two colleagues arriving here in Mexico next week. Hired a car service to meet them at the airport with a sign. That's fine. A nice gesture. If my best friend was coming though, I'd take the bus an hour to the airport. I'd arrive early. I'd wait for him at the exit with a sign that had his name on it and a pic from *Mega Man X*, the game we played together as kids. Then we'd take a taxi back into town together.

The airport test, I now call it. Somebody you know is arriving on an early morning flight. Of course, they can grab a cab from the airport. Do you pick them up?

Logic isn't the point. Effort is. True friendship isn't passive. It acts. The second proxy is needless effort.

And the final proxy of true friendship is whether somebody will celebrate with you. There are likely lots of people you can call to commiserate with you when things are bad. It's harder to find somebody that is genuinely happy for you when things go well.

In summary, you've got a true friend if they pass these three tests:

1. **Uselessness.** They do nothing for your professional or social ambitions.
2. **Effort.** They go out of their way for you even if it doesn't make sense, just because.
3. **Celebration.** They are genuinely happy for you when things go well.

THE TRUE FRIEND TEST

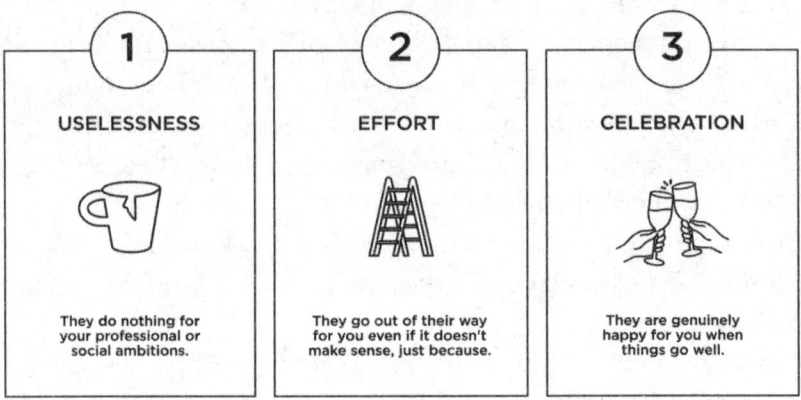

The three-parts of the true friend test are uselessness (they serve no practical purpose), effort (they go out of their way without reason), and celebration (they genuinely rejoice in your success). The ironic thing is that the truest friends we have are people we don't actually need yet who are essential. (©Unhinged Habits)

A reader, Nina, in response to an email I sent, asked me a good question.

"I had a friendship that I thought was grounded in virtue, but for my 'friend,' it seems to now be grounded in utility. This mismatch sucks. What do you think about these situations?"

I told Nina that my first instinct is that this isn't a friendship grounded in virtue any longer. While some friends come and go, more often friendships shift.

True friends can be defined best as being excessively useless. Nobody gains anything that they can quantify or qualify, and yet it's the most special thing. The moment a friend becomes useful, it's no longer grounded in virtue. Just as a garden changes with the seasons, so does your social life.

True friendship is fundamentally an act of service. You have to learn how to be a friend before you can make a friend. Maintaining one is hard. It takes time. Time none of us have enough of with our ambitions and families and the pace of our hectic lives.

This means going first. Putting yourself out there, showing vulnerability, inviting them to stuff, reaching out, following up, and understanding that life gets busy, but a true friend is with you over the ebbs and flows of

The Joy of Fewer Friends

it all. Sometimes long stretches of time will pass where you don't see one another and that's okay too.

My one true friend, Andrew, and I don't talk often. Whenever we do, it's like we're continuing a conversation we had yesterday, even if there's a year in between. We talk about important things, and we talk about unimportant things.

You know that wildly inappropriate (or probably not funny) joke that pops in your head? The one that you usually don't say because you're with an acquaintance and aren't sure whether they'd laugh or never want to see you again.

With a true friend, you say it. Like this one:

Why do ducks have feathers?

To cover their butt quacks!

No matter how fowl the wise-quack is, with a true friend, bad jokes are better than good jokes. When your buddy tells a bad joke you get to make fun of him for how lame it was and that's actually more enjoyable for both of you than hearing a good joke.

Flowers, like acquaintances, are a pleasant happenstance. A giant tree, like a true friend, is worth going out of your way to see.

It doesn't matter if you talk to a true friend every day or once a year. There's a mutual understanding that people can just have stuff going on. You can go for long periods of time without talking. But when you reconnect, it's as good as ever.

Having too many of the wrong types of friends weighs you down the same as an excess of belongings. Unlike with buying too much stuff, however, you can't buy a bigger house to store friends in. Time's finite. You and I have the same twenty-four hours. With relationships, sadly, we all have the same tiny home.

"A lot of the reason we look to friends is because they're a source of meaning. If you're getting meaning in other ways (like with work, for the time being), it's easy to let your friendships wither. That's one reason success can be isolating," wrote Hank Green. Money and prestige tend to shrink available time for friends. If you discover that too much of your time is taken up by deal friends, you're not alone. These friendships do have utility but tend to leave us unfulfilled.

Unhinged Habits

Sure, go for a drink with colleagues after work. But don't forget to also call your buddy. And, if you have the time to do only one, skip the work thing. As Arthur Brooks says, "cancel on your deal friends for your real friends."

Go ahead and maintain friendships of all types. But research from the University of Michigan indicates that the number of friends we have doesn't meaningfully impact our well-being. Instead, all you need for higher levels of life satisfaction, self-esteem, and lower levels of depression are two relationships: a spouse and one true friendship.

When it comes to adult friendship, the quality and depth of your friendships are more crucial to mental health than sheer numbers.

Andrew is my one true friend.

We grew up on the same street. My house number was 191, his 95. I still have his family's home phone number memorized from when we were eight: 512-0619.

There's been as long as two-year stints where we didn't speak. But if he ever needed anything, I'd drop everything and hop on a plane.

Friendships, however, don't have to be deep and cultivated to positively contribute to your social ecosystem.

I want to talk about the birds in your garden a bit more. That's because, in a digital age, the friction cost of making or breaking a relationship approaches zero.

PARASOCIAL RELATIONSHIPS

Swipe left. "Heart" a post. Respond to DMs. Living online means living in a constant state of diversion. Always something else. Always *someone* else. And whatever the else is always seems more interesting, more compelling, and more attractive in the moment.

Convenience has brought with it the loss of deep engagement.

- We call an Uber instead of asking a buddy for a ride.
- We celebrate a win on social media instead of going to a loved one for that same validation.
- We do a video launch party for our new venture instead of renting the local pub.

The Joy of Fewer Friends

Technological freedom is a vast ocean of infinite options and infinite connection. A soothing Band-Aid of false intimacy that optimizes interaction out of our lives. Despite having more "friends" than ever, our society is dying of loneliness.

But it's not all bad.

Parasocial friends—one-sided relationships where a person feels a sense of connection, emotional investment, or familiarity with another who doesn't know them personally (typically a public figure, celebrity, or fictional character)—can be both healthy and emotionally fulfilling.

Content creators, YouTubers, authors, and actors require no investment. They're entertaining. Can act as welcome distractions. And, unlike casual friends where all this awkward stuff happens like wondering whether you're saying the right thing or if they like you, there's no social risk.

In the TV era, parasocial relationships existed with fictional characters acting out a role. "People would become a Tom Cruise fan and obsess over Tom Cruise," said Mark Manson. "When really, all you did was see him in *Risky Business* and *Top Gun*. You know nothing about the guy. He turned out to be a head case and nobody knew."

Maybe you're not getting the full authentic version of an influencer now, but you are getting some facet of their personality. In this way, social media is a marked improvement over television or film.

It's easy to make fun of parasocial relationships. To be the old man shaking his fist shouting at kids from his porch, saying "Back in my day we used to leave the house to see our friends."

Times have changed. These relationships, while sometimes toxic, can be a healthy way to have a sense of belonging—a safe and easy way to make you feel seen. Fulfilling you in ways unavailable from people who happen to be nearby.

The positive is also the negative.

Because parasocial relationships are so easy, the ceiling on them is low. It's easy to get in, get your dose, and escape. As a result, the satisfaction you get early on is probably as much as you're ever going to get. Contrast this with deep and meaningful relationships that tend to get better over time with no limit.

INFLUENCERS VERSUS REAL FRIENDS

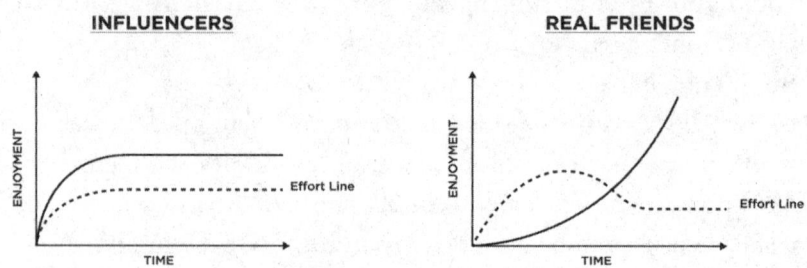

Parasocial relationships are one-sided connections with content creators, celebrities, or fictional characters who don't know you exist. While offering risk-free entertainment and a sense of belonging without social awkwardness, these easy relationships are nice but come with a ceiling—their initial satisfaction is likely their peak, unlike real friendships that deepen endlessly over time. (©Unhinged Habits)

One-sided online friendships are fine as a supplement to your social life, so long as they don't replace it.

The danger comes when digital connections crowd out face-to-face ones, or when the dopamine hit of online interaction becomes more appealing than the sometimes messy work of real-world friendship.

A simple habit stack I've found useful: when you catch yourself doom-scrolling, consciously switch to texting a friend to say hello. Convert the digital impulse into real-world connection. Go from scroll to soul.

You might even connect with other "bird watchers" who share your interests. When two people bond over their shared appreciation for the same content creator, podcast host, or public figure, they're forming an authentic connection through a mutual interest. Parasocial relationships can actually become the connective tissue between real people.

Like the time last week when a writer who followed the same newsletter as I do was visiting Mexico for a wedding. I sent a car to pick him up. We hiked and talked about writing, writing as a career, and building an authorship profile on the internet. This guy is obsessed in the way I am, a way that my wife and best friend aren't.

Your Garden of Friendship isn't static of course. It transforms with the seasons of your life, sometimes in surprising ways.

CIRCUMSTANCES CHANGE, PEOPLE CHANGE

Ten of us were tight in high school. Girls and guys. We'd hang every weekend together. We knew each other's secrets, finished each other's sentences, made out at parties, and pretended it didn't happen the next day.

College scattered us. Some to the same schools. Others far away. Summer brought us back together. Three guys from the group even married three of the girls.

After graduation we lived close enough. Saw each other sometimes. Then came marriages. Kids. Houses. Toronto real estate prices pushed us out in different directions. East. North. West.

Those who bought houses near each other still hang out. The rest of us don't. We like posts on social media; comment occasionally.

I think about my high school friends often. They shaped me. In a way, I miss them. But circumstances changed. They changed. I changed.

We did start one tradition in high school that I'm grateful for. A yearly Christmakah dinner during the holidays. We all meet up for a meal and catch up. It's been going on for twenty-four years.

Seeing everyone is wonderful. But what's jarring is how unfamiliar these people have become. I don't know them anymore. I wouldn't even recognize many of them on the street if we walked past one another. Which makes sense. I see them only once a year.

I love these people. I really do. But life moves on. They've moved on. I've moved on. I accept that. But I'm still happy we rekindle what we once had, once a year, you know, for old times' sake.

Major life transitions sort our relationships quickly. A new city reveals which friendships had convenience at their core and which had something deeper. A baby shows which childless friends adapt to your new reality and which fade away.

This evolution isn't tragic. It's the natural rhythm of connection throughout a lifetime. The key is seeing it happen and deciding which relationships deserve your fight to maintain, and which ones you let transform or wither away.

Unhinged Habits

Not all friendships are meant to last forever. Some serve their purpose and naturally fade. Others require intentional pruning. The challenge is knowing which to let go gracefully and which to fight for.

When a friendship no longer serves you, remember: ghosting isn't a strategy, it's avoidance. Instead, try the "slow fade with occasional warmth." Gradually reduce contact, but when you do connect, be genuinely present. This allows relationships to naturally find their appropriate level of engagement.

For friendships worth fighting for that have drifted, try the "specific memory reconnect." Don't just text "We should catch up sometime." Instead, reference a specific shared experience: "Remember when we stayed up all night debating whether *Mega Man 2* or *Mega Man X* was the best Mega Man game? I had that argument again yesterday and thought of you. Free for coffee next Tuesday?"

Ending old friendships isn't failure; it's making room. And building new ones isn't about first impressions; it's about creating shared stories.

STEVE THE MAILMAN

You know what we need?

We need to bring back actual community. Accountability. Connection. We need to actually know our neighbors again. To opt in to people close to us instead of wiling away our time in anonymity in a digital world.

Steve's my mailman. He doesn't just deliver my mail. He smiles, I wave. We chat.

Pretty soon we won't need mailpeople. Drones can do the job. Cuts costs, builds efficiency. No sick days, HR, or unions.

It'll be a shame when that happens. If we ignore these less definable sources of value, we commit what I've heard referred to as the "doorman fallacy." Machines can open doors, yet fancy buildings still have doormen. That's because, in addition to door opening, doormen signal the status of the hotel, discourage vagrants, give directions, and provide a hint of recognition to people returning home.

I look forward to seeing Steve.

The Joy of Fewer Friends

He's a friendly face. Part of my community. The more jobs like his that are displaced by technology, the more static and uninteresting my day will become. Grayscale, all color removed in the single-minded pursuit of efficiency and profit.

I've lived in paradise—luxury, at the top of a hill overlooking exotic beaches of Thailand, a mansion on the Pacific Ocean on the North Shore of Oahu, and an off-the-grid eco-home on a remote beach in Uruguay.

I'm happiest when I'm living close to others in a community.

Living in a Mexican *pueblecito* taught me that it's okay to romanticize about paradise. To dream about a huge house with acres of land to roam. An infinity pool to skinny dip in. The scent of fresh hibiscus wafting through the open-air kitchen. Cucumber-infused water. But I know the truth: those things are nice for short-term vacations. For a getaway, not every day.

Every day is best lived in proximity to others.

Every day is best lived inside a vibrant community.

Our home is the corner house of a walkable community. It has two big side yards. One with a fence, one without. In the summertime, our kids play on the one without the fence. I read, Alison does art on Muskoka chairs on our driveway. We say hi to people passing by.

Maximizing your daily positive microinteractions with acquaintants leads to a marked improvement in quality of life.

The shared smile with a neighbor, hello from a mailman, wave of recognition to the clerk at the store . . . All little moments, not meaningful by themselves, add up. All flowers in your garden. Fine without, better with. These frequent interactions, in aggregate, influence your mood more positively than even your closest friends and family members can. Paying a bit extra for your bagels at Fred's bakery is a good deal if it means you get to see Fred.

My rich buddies are always talking about taxes. How to pay less, specifically. Many of them have moved away from friends and community to a low-tax state or tax-free country. In almost every case, at great financial and time and energy expense, they return home after a few years.

"Something was missing," they say.

Unhinged Habits

On paper, they moved to pay less tax. What they learned the hard way is that everybody pays the same taxes; they just pay in different ways.

When we live abroad, we don't rent the big house on the hill overlooking the ocean.

Instead, we find a complex with twenty to forty condos and a big pool. Then we try to rent the unit on the ground floor either right by the pool or in the middle of the main walking artery. We sit on our balcony. Alison does art projects with the kids. (Papier-mâché dinosaurs last year.) And there's balloons. There's always balloons. Life doesn't suck *without* balloons. But life is better *with* balloons. Same as flowers. As people walk by, we say hi or *hola* or *sawadee ka* or whatever. They respond. We invite them and their kids to join. That's how we build community when we live abroad.

"Social wealth is built upon a foundation of depth—upon the strength of your ties to these few, cherished relationships. It is expanded through breadth—connection to extended circles of friends, communities, and culture," wrote Sahil Bloom in *The 5 Types of Wealth*.

Here's a few more examples of how to build relationship breadth:

Alison hosts a "ladies lunch" once or twice a year. She invites eight to ten other women who live close by. Many of whom don't know one another (and some of them Alison doesn't know well). They order Thai food.

We host a Halloween party every year. It's big. 150 people. Halloween's fun, but trick-or-treating is over so quickly. Alison chooses a day the weekend before Halloween, designs a flyer, and sends it to people we know. Then we post it at the park inviting all neighbors.

For a month before the event, crafting with the kids is making carnival games out of cardboard from deliveries. I buy terrible Canadian coffee that all of us are genetically predisposed to enjoy from Tim Hortons, Calvin makes pots of hot chocolate, and we draw a Snakes and Ladders board with chalk on the driveway. People we know come. But people we don't know also come. Last year a family showed up. They bought a house a few streets away and hadn't moved in yet. They said that they were doing a walk-through and saw the sign for our party at the park.

You might find yourself in a place with challenging cultural differences. That can be hard. When we lived in Montenegro, Alison found the other families and kids standoffish. She'd make eye contact, smile, say *zdravo*, and get ignored.

One day, she brought bubbles to the park. Kids ran to the bubbles. Other parents came with their kids. The other families weren't unfriendly, simply reserved. Different cultures are different, but humans are humans.

What I've discovered through living in various countries is that friendship operates on different timetables across cultures.

- North Americans tend to form quick, seemingly deep connections that often remain somewhat surface level.
- Northern Europeans typically take longer to warm up but form more enduring bonds once established.
- In many Asian and Latin American cultures, friendship often intertwines with family connections and obligations in ways that Westerners might find initially overwhelming.

The key isn't mastering every cultural norm but recognizing when you're experiencing a different friendship "language" and adjusting your expectations accordingly.

If there's one thing I've learned from more than a decade of travel, it's that just about every human is a wonderful person if you take the time to get to know them. Bubbles broke down the cultural barrier and transformed the energy at the park. From that day forward, for three months in Montenegro, Alison kept bubbles in her purse.

I guess what I'm saying is that the two secrets to social wealth are bubbles and balloons. That's it. That's the book. I could end it here. More bubbles. More balloons. Maybe throw in a game of freeze tag. There you have it. We're done talking. It's true what Robert Fulghum said, everything you need to know you learned in kindergarten.

Alison's the MVP. Wives always are.

She'll want to knit. Suddenly, I'll see eight people in a knitting circle on our driveway.

Activities are often better when done with others. Even if you don't know the others well. Especially if you don't know the others well. Because then you get the added benefit of getting to know the others.

Unhinged Habits

Three to five ladies work out in our garage twice a week. It's informal. All fitness levels. Joanne started to come this year. She'd just retired; her kids are grown up. Jaden bumps around. He's two. Joanne invited him to bake muffins after a workout one day. It's become a regular thing. Jaden brings some home to me each time. I like the muffins. They're blueberry.

Everybody, everywhere, wants to be connected. Most people never make time to connect. You can change that. How wonderful.

A person doesn't need to consume you to have been worthwhile. Sometimes you have friends where the only bond you have is time, temporary location, fleeting interest, or circumstance. Long relationships may be richer, but relatively brief, relatively uncomplicated encounters with humans who happen to be sharing space alongside you can be nice too.

Call them acquaintances. They're friends but friends of convenience. These are people you didn't choose but people who happen to surround you. Neighbors, shopkeepers, mailmen; the guy who walks his dogs at the same time every day that you always see so you assume he lives nearby. It's people that you recognize. People you're doing this life thing in parallel with.

They're worth getting to know.

Think about your own Garden of Friendship. Where are you investing your limited time and energy?

Fill in the names of people in your life in the chart below. Categorize the people in your life so you can properly assess where your energy is being spent and how you might be able to better invest it.

Your Garden of Friendship inventory

Birds (one-sided / parasocial)	Grass (utility / colleagues)	Flowers (acquaintances / community)	Trees (true friend(s))

The Joy of Fewer Friends

Next, a few reflection questions

- What one friendship deserves your greatest level of attention?
  _____
  _____

- What specific action could you take this week to invest in it?
  _____
  _____
  _____
  _____

- If you made a list of the five people you spend the most time with and a separate list of the five people who bring you the most joy, how much overlap would there be? What does this reveal about where your time and energy are currently going?
  _____
  _____
  _____
  _____

You can download an expanded friendship inventory chart complete with reflection questions at www.Jonathangoodman.com/friends.

Unhinged Habits

At some point in your childhood, you and your friends went outside to play for the last time and nobody knew it.

How much would you pay to go back to that exact moment? Why not just make the choices that you'd make then, now? Should you really be trading all your best hours for money?

Sometimes we miss an entire season of life we could have participated in just because we didn't realize we were participating in it until it was gone. One day the season will just be over. There's no warning sign. It's just done. And that's usually the point where you wish there was a way to know you were in the good old days before you've actually left them.

True friend(s) provide what no amount of success, money, or achievement ever could: the profound comfort in being known and loved for who you truly are.

There's a few key points we can pull out here:

First, it's totally okay to categorize your friends.

Next, invest in your local community.

And finally, if you've found a true friend, cherish them. Maybe even put down this book and give them a call. Or, better yet, invite them for tacos. You know, just to shoot the shit or whatever.

Next, the best advice Mom ever gave me. It's about love.

CHAPTER 6 SUMMARY

- **Identify your true friend(s) using the three proxies.** True friends are those who are useless to your ambitions, make needless effort on your behalf, and genuinely celebrate your successes. These relationships exist outside utility and convenience. If you've found one, cherish them.

- **Cancel on your deal friends for your real friends.** When faced with competing social commitments, prioritize connections of depth over those of utility. The relationships that transform your life rarely advance your career.

- **Build a daily community through microinteractions.** Maximize small, positive exchanges with neighbors, shopkeepers, and service people. These seemingly insignificant connections, in aggregate, contribute significantly to life satisfaction.

- **Balance your social ecosystem intentionally.** Distinguish between parasocial relationships, deal friends, acquaintances, and true friends. Then deliberately allocate your limited time and energy toward those who matter most.

7.

Find Your Missing Half

Grow separate to become stronger than the sum of your parts.

When Alison graduated from naturopathic medical school and left for Thailand, I didn't plan to follow her. Then Mom called.

"Jon, if you love her, you better get your ass on a plane."

I booked a flight that night.

In this chapter, I'll show you why the most successful relationships aren't built on similarity but on complementarity. That differences, when respected and leveraged, create a relationship stronger than the sum of its parts.

We're drawn to people like us, yet ironically, it's our differences that make relationships thrive.

You'll discover why growing apart in healthy ways actually strengthens your bond. And then I'll introduce you to the 4S Celebration Protocol, a framework that will transform how you approach meaningful work by bringing the people you love into your journey.

Before we begin, a note:

I heard somebody say that if you think you understand love, you don't. And I believe that to be true.

Maybe that's why anything deep you say about it sounds cheesy.

Unhinged Habits

I am in love. Truly. Madly. And deeply. It feels almost impossible. Still, I'm not going to pretend that I've even come close to solving this thing. Instead, just want to share a few bits and pieces I've figured out.

The happiest couples round out each other's personality.
They don't read the same books or have the same friends.
One can be introverted, the other extroverted.
One a night person, the other useless after sunset. Or, in my case, 11:00 a.m.
You need compatibility, but, like, not all that much. More than anything, you need complementarity, shared values, and respect for the other person's individuality.

I like mornings, Alison doesn't. Most days, I make breakfast and get the kids ready while she lies in bed and gets going slowly. She comes down the stairs, and there's food on the table and the school bags are packed. But, then, I'm useless in the evening. She does the bedtime routine, and I show up to read books.

I'm sure that me not helping at night frustrates her sometimes. Same as some mornings I wish she lent more of a hand. It's a good thing our energy patterns are different though. House management would be hard otherwise. Imagine if both of us were morning people? Nighttimes would be a drag.

Hobbies . . . interests . . . the pace of your life—this will all change. "Marriage," David Brooks wrote, "starts in rhapsodies and ends in carpools."

Getting married is crazy bold. One person to do life with. It's an insane proposal. Then you face the real job, which is taking off your mask and being with somebody who has taken off theirs.

"Before you are married, you can live under the illusion that you are easy to live with. But to be married is to volunteer for the most thorough surveillance program known to mankind," wrote Alain de Botton. It's the stripping off of the idealized projection. The disillusion that follows is inevitable. Be with somebody long enough, and you'll learn who they really are . . . and who you really are.

I'm starting to figure out what love means.

It's a difficult balance of intimacy and independence that is not always wildly passionate. Don't get me wrong, the butterflies still exist—just fewer and farther between. The highs aren't crazy high anymore, but the lows disappear.

Love is more of a gentle warmth. A warm cup of coffee on a cold Sunday morning when you've got nowhere to rush to. It's that moment when you hold on to a hug an extra few seconds, press your fingers into that fleshy spot between her shoulder blades; the look and smile and double-pump squeeze of the hand you're holding as you watch your child being kind to another kid. Love is the feeling you get seconds before walking through the door, knowing she's inside.

When you really love someone, it's serene.

See, told you. Anything deep you write about love sounds cheesy.

LOVE'S PROGRESSION FROM INTENSITY TO SERENITY

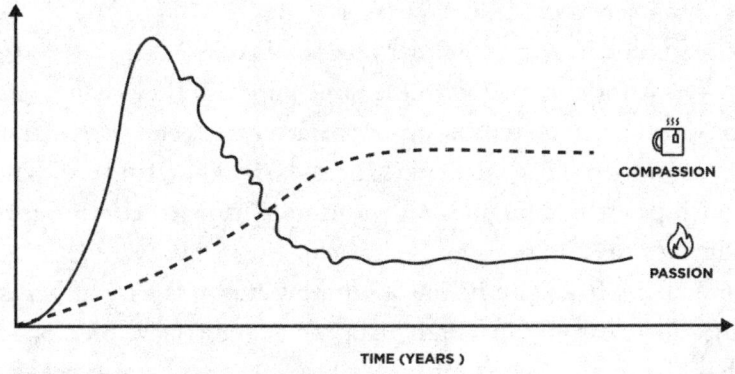

As relationships mature, passion, while still there, takes a back seat to compassion. The initial fiery rhapsody evolves into more of a balanced and serene intimacy. (Adapted from *The Anxious Generation* by Jonathan Haidt)

I thought that I loved Alison when we got married. I said the word. But I didn't know what it meant. That wasn't love. That was lust. That was passion.

Passion peaks when you're young, but love is the thing that peaks in old age. In order for that to happen, you need to let down your guard. To take off your mask. To admit your imperfections. When you're forced to make it work with another human, something wonderful happens—it works, because the other person does the same, and you both discover that where you lack, they don't. That magically, almost impossibly, you complete one another. So much so that it feels weird when you're confronted with the obvious truth that you are, in fact, different people.

A SMORGASBORD OF SAMENESS

Restlessness in a relationship tends to be founded on agreeableness rather than affection. Dating technology and an algorithmically fueled online life has removed serendipity and randomness from the process.

Eighty-five percent of millennials on a dating website said that how a potential date votes is extremely important to them. We don't just swipe away pictures if we don't deem a person attractive enough. It's deeper than that. We don't even *see* their picture if their profile doesn't list the same music, hobbies, and political views as us.

You shouldn't be searching for a version of yourself.

Don't look for a partner with the same hobbies. They change. Instead, look for somebody who matches your character traits and values. Traits like cleanliness, work ethic, generosity. Values like family, friends, and lifestyle. Relationships are codependent. Two unique humans coming together. Forming a team. Ambitions mutually held.

Remember what I said before about how Alison is a night person and I'm a morning person. On a dating app we wouldn't have met. She'd have listed hobbies that occur at night. Maybe would have wanted to see a concert that extended [gasp] past 10:00 p.m. As if that's a real time that people experience vertically.

The very difference that helps us manage our household is the exact sort of thing that, on a dating website, might have stopped us from finding one another in the first place.

An example of shared values with different personalities: Alison and I both value friendship, but it manifests differently.

She's extroverted; I'm introverted. She's a planner; I'm not.

I'm happy to go along with plans but rarely make them.

Alison doesn't have to consult with me to invite people over or make plans on nights and weekends. She is 100 percent in charge of our social calendar.

If, in the rare case, I have something going (a work thing, seeing my one friend, playing tennis with a neighbor, whatever), I let her know. It's less about asking permission. More about one partner owning that part of our shared lives, accepting the responsibility and cognitive load of it because it better suits their personality.

Another example: family finances.

We both studied money and wealth for sixty days. Then we agreed on what our family's philosophical approach was toward spending money, accruing wealth, accepting risk, and making investments. She then handed off the management of our money to me.

Nothing's hidden from Alison. But I accept both the responsibility and cognitive load of our family's financial well-being. If I want to do something, I don't need to ask permission. Instead, I fill her in. When she wanted to buy a few rental houses with a joint venture partner, it was the same as if I were to book a weekend hangout with friends: totally fine, but clear it with the other person who manages that aspect of our shared lives so that they can plan accordingly.

"Some similarity in basic values is no doubt beneficial to a partnership, but too much sameness brings huge costs," wrote Arthur Brooks. "Romantic love requires complementarity—that is, differences." Loving, long-lasting relationships, especially ones that withstand the pressures of children, aging parents, and careers, require tremendous trust and, with that, a delineation of responsibilities.

Here's a few questions for you to reflect on:

1. In what specific ways do you and your partner complement rather than mirror each other?
2. How have these differences strengthened your relationship?

Unhinged Habits

You can download a worksheet to map you and your partner's strengths, helping you recognize and leverage each other's natural competencies at www.Jonathangoodman.com/partner.

Complementarity isn't just about fitting together like puzzle pieces. It's about creating space for each other to grow. Strong partnerships demand that both people develop themselves independently to strengthen what they build together.

LIFT YOUR OWN WEIGHT

The loneliest period of my life was a trip to New Zealand after a semester abroad in Australia.

Before flying home, with my last eighteen New Zealand dollars, I bought a small piece of jade and saved it for six years.

I gave it to Alison the day that I said "I love you" to her for the first time. She's worn it around her neck ever since.

Sixteen years after that trip, on April 1, 2022, at 4:33 a.m., she gave birth to our second son, Jaden Goodman.

Earlier in this book, we met Alice Lemée near the end of her Season of Yes in New York City. I promised you the other half of her story. Here it is:

She was in love with a man in New York. But a part of her felt unfulfilled. He couldn't leave. She felt she needed to. They broke up. She left.

Found herself. Then she came home. Got back together with him. They're in love, now more than ever.

"People think a spouse will make you feel whole, but they won't. You must become whole yourself, first. A partner is the cherry on top, not the sundae," she told me. Then she added, "We want others to be the answer to our dissatisfaction."

Later, in an article titled "We Break Our Own Hearts," Alice wrote:

Some walks you have to take alone.

If you decide to go down that path, brace yourself: It's going to put you through an unimaginable amount of pain. But I promise—pinky-swear—the clouds will part.

And once they do, you'll access a massive reservoir of self-love and confidence. That version of you on the other side will embrace you with open arms and be so glad you made it.

And as for your relationship? If it's meant to be, it will be. Because if it's true love, you two will find your way back to one another, and you'll return to them a more well-rounded person. That's a gift to both them and you.

Enjoy different hobbies. Travel. Explore. Don't be afraid to evolve, or for your spouse to evolve. Stagnation is unattractive. Forms moss. In order for you to grow together, each partner needs to grow apart.

"What, indeed, is love if not the enmeshing of separate excitements?" wrote Maria Popova. Alison does art. I write books. I don't knit or have any desire to knit. She doesn't write books, nor do we talk much about the books that I write.

My opinion is that she's the prettiest, coolest, most clever knitter ever. Her opinion is that I'm the wittiest, coolest, and most handsome writer ever. We don't have to know all about knitting or writing to form these opinions.

Some things we share, like fitness, and others we don't. Not overlapping means we always have stuff to talk about—uncomplicated by personal investment, devoid of competition. As Lydia Netzer wrote, "We can still support each other without being all in the other person's stuff. Doing your own thing, having your own friends, being completely insanely passionate about something that the other person has no idea, really, about, is awesome."

When we lived in Uruguay, Alison traveled to Peru for an ayahuasca ceremony in the jungle for three weeks. I went to Rio De Janeiro to hang with some guys I knew who were living there.

We were both coming to life in new ways, becoming aware of deep character traits we never reckoned with before. Her energetically, me experientially. Trusting that the other person was discovering themselves in profound ways that they'd bring back to our relationship as we continue to do this life thing, together.

In order to live a life together, you've got to learn how to live your own. To lift your own weights.

There's a saying I like, which is that sameness attracts but newness keeps us together. It's true that most days are the same. But occasionally, there's one of marked contrast. You cannot lose that. Call it the first rule of getting through life: you have to care about something other than yourself or the person you're with.

Independence and togetherness are complementary, not opposite. True independence gives you something worth bringing back to the relationship. And meaningful togetherness gives you the foundation to venture out on your own.

When you lift your own weight, you develop strengths that enrich your partnership. When you celebrate together, you create the emotional bonds that make independence feel safe, not threatening. The strongest relationships have this rhythm: growing separate, coming together. Celebrating. Growing separate. Coming together. Celebrating. It's a dance you both do. Let me show you how.

CELEBRATING DIFFERENCES, TOGETHER

The test for whether something matters is whether it makes you a better human for having done it. Part of that is whether or not it brings you closer to the people that you love as a result.

Find Your Missing Half

The people who love you want to celebrate with you but don't know how. Left to their own devices, they'll wait for a positive outcome—a job promotion, the sale of a business, an award—and celebrate after the fact. But it's the process they should be celebrating, not the outcome. However, it's not your loved one's responsibility to figure out when and how to celebrate. It's yours.

A simple way to add richness to personal or professional growth is to design shared experiences at waypoints that signify process wins along the way of achieving individual goals.

An example from my previous book.

The day after submitting the first draft to my editor, I took my family on a trip to the two-volcano island of Ometepe.

The day after submitting the second draft for a full edit, I met my dad for a week in Oaxaca City.

The day after submitting the final manuscript, Alison and I enjoyed a romantic getaway in Quimixto.

All of these events were scheduled far in advance. In some cases, I self-imposed a deadline, told my editor, and scheduled a trip for the day after. The book was something I did by myself. The process was made richer by celebrating it with others.

These experiences follow a structured framework anyone can use I call the 4S Celebration Protocol. It works because it:

- creates anticipation (a powerful motivator),
- strengthens relationships (providing emotional support during challenges), and
- acknowledges effort rather than just outcomes (building intrinsic motivation).

Most importantly, it ensures you're experiencing joy throughout your journey, not just at the end.

For every important project in your life, identify two to three key milestones along your journey, and complete this sentence for each:

Unhinged Habits

After I _____, I will _____,

with _____.

You'll need to first define each milestone with clear "done" criteria. Building a meditation routine, for example, is too vague. Instead, specify something like "meditating for twenty minutes for twenty consecutive days." (I've included examples next to help you get started.)

From there, design meaningful celebrations that follows the 4S's:

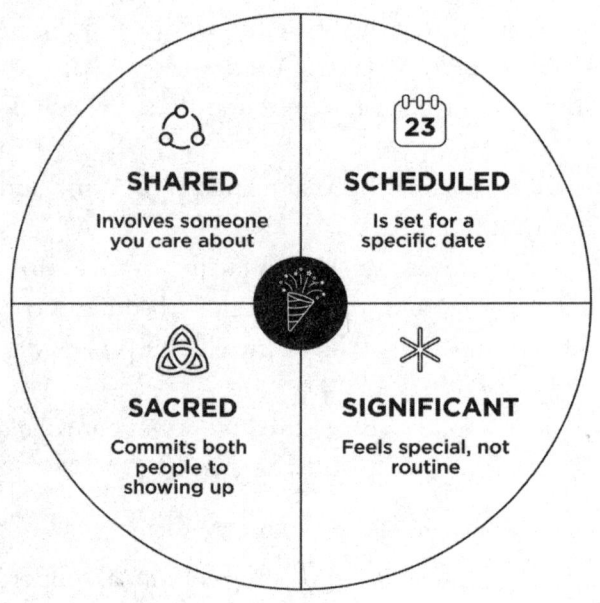

Shared–Involves someone you care about

Scheduled–Is set for a specific date

Sacred–Commits both people to showing up

Significant–Feels special, not routine

This protocol embodies intentional life design at its core. It creates structures that align your actions with your values. It ensures the journey itself becomes rewarding. And it's a way to celebrate the growth and differences that bring people together.

Here's some examples for different types of goals:

For career growth:
- After submitting twenty job applications → Special dinner with a mentor
- After completing five networking interviews → Nature hike with a parent

For health goals
- After thirty days of 80 percent adherence to a structured exercise plan → Spa day with a friend
- After testing ten new healthy recipes → Host a small dinner party with neighbors

For creative projects
- After compiling fifty specific research sources/references → Museum visit with a creative partner
- After finishing the outline/blueprint phase → Live music or comedy show with your spouse

For personal development
- After completing all modules in your online course → Weekend trip with family
- After your first public speaking engagement → Lunch with your spouse

This protocol works for tiny milestones as well. Specifically, actions you are either procrastinating about or areas where you want to establish a habit. Use these sparingly, but they can be useful.

Unhinged Habits

Tiny milestones

- After completing twenty days of daily writing → Coffee date at bookstore with writing friend
- After sending three difficult emails you've been putting off sending → Evening walk and ice cream with your spouse

For each project you take on, whether it's professional or personal, it is helpful to fill out this quick chart. Some projects will have more milestones than others. I've found that three is the max. More than that and they begin to lose their specialness. But some can have fewer.

This protocol works whether your project spans weeks, months, or years.

For shorter projects, you might have just one midpoint celebration. For bigger projects, two or maybe three. The key is spacing celebrations so they provide regular psychological rewards without losing their special significance.

Here's what my chart looked like for my previous book:

Milestone	Done Criteria	Celebration	With Whom	By When
First draft of book	Submitted to editor	Four days in Ometepe	Family	Feb. 2, 2024
Second draft of book	Submitted to editor	Week in Oaxaca City	Dad	Feb. 26, 2024
Final manuscript	Submitted to editor	Romantic weekend getaway in Quimixto	Alison	March 24, 2024

Another example, for a friend who was transitioning careers:

Milestone	Done Criteria	Celebration	With Whom	By When
Résumé / skills update	Updated résumé and LinkedIn profile, and completed two skill certification courses	Weekend hiking trip	True friend	March 15, 2025
Application campaign	Submitted applications to twenty-five companies in new target industry	Dinner at that new fancy sushi joint that just opened	Spouse	May 1, 2025
Interview milestone	Completed five second-round interviews	Wine tasting tour at local vineyard	Former mentor who encouraged career change	June 20, 2025

And one more for a friend of a friend who told her personal trainer about this, and they built it out alongside one another:

Milestone	Done Criteria	Celebration	With Whom	By When
Establishing consistency	Completed first thirty days of the planned exercise routine with an 80 percent success rate	Couples massage	Spouse	April 10, 2025
Strength benchmark	First unassisted pull-up or deadlifting bodyweight	Shopping trip for new workout gear	True friend	May 15, 2025

Unhinged Habits

Milestone	Done Criteria	Celebration	With Whom	By When
Completion of initial program	Finished twelve-week program with 80 percent adherence	Weekend trip to nearby lake	Family	June 3, 2025

To help you apply the 4S Celebration Protocol, you can download additional examples and a chart at www.Jonathangoodman.com/4s.

When I teach this protocol, a few common challenges arise. I'll call them out because you might be thinking the same thing:

"My project has no clear milestones." Break it down further. Every project can be divided into stages. If you're struggling, ask, "What would need to happen for me to feel 25 percent done, 50 percent done?"

"My celebrations feel forced." Choose activities that genuinely excite you. The celebration should feel like a reward, not another obligation. Something outside of your regular routine. An afternoon in nature. Fancy latte at bougie coffee spot. Foot massages in Chinatown.

"The other person isn't as excited as I am." Be explicit about why this milestone matters to you. Share your journey so they understand what they're celebrating. Or don't even tell them. You can enjoy time with one another as a celebration, even if they don't know the reason.

But, by far, the biggest objection I hear is **"I'm afraid to tell people about my goals."** This fear is valid and backed by research.

When we publicly announce our intentions, we sometimes experience a premature sense of accomplishment that reduces our motivation to actually complete the task.

My solution: Don't tell people why you're scheduling the celebration in advance. Simply book the special time with them without explaining its significance.

You know the milestone it's connected to; they don't need to know until you've already achieved it. When you meet for the celebration, you can share your accomplishment and why you wanted to mark this specific moment together.

This approach maintains accountability to yourself while avoiding the potential demotivating effects of premature goal-sharing.

THE 4S CELEBRATION PROTOCOL
FOR ENJOYING THE PROCESS

The 4S Celebration Protocol transforms challenging projects into meaningful journeys by anchoring key milestones to shared experiences with people you care about. It allows you to celebrate differences, and growth, alongside the people that you love. (©Unhinged Habits)

People who love you want to support your career and your passions. These people will rarely shout the loudest to demand your attention. Time passes, and if you're not careful, you'll end up neglecting them—the very people who want the best for you. And then, even a win feels empty.

It's up to you to include people in your process.

It's up to you to invite people you love into your world.

So, celebrate outcomes, sure.

But also make sure to celebrate the process, together.

That way, regardless of the outcome *this time*, it's a win before the result shows itself. If it ever shows itself.

Okay, we've covered a lot already, you and I. There's one last thing we need to talk about: Freedom.

CHAPTER 7 SUMMARY

- **Divide responsibilities based on natural strengths.** Agree on a philosophical approach and trust your partner to manage aspects of your shared life like finances, social calendars, or childcare routines where they excel, reducing daily friction and eliminating the need for constant negotiation over every decision.

- **Seek complementarity, not similarity.** The strongest relationships aren't built on shared interests or matching personalities but on differences that balance and complete each other. Look for compatible values and character traits, not hobbies, daily rhythms, or social preferences.

- **Lift your own weight.** True love requires each person to pursue their own growth and bring something unique back to the relationship. Develop separate interests, take solo adventures, or cultivate skills your partner doesn't.

- **Use the 4S Celebration Protocol to share your journey.** Schedule meaningful experiences with loved ones at key milestones throughout your process, not just at the finish line of a project. Design celebrations that are shared, scheduled, sacred, and significant to add richness into the journey.

8.

The Profound Power of Ruthlessly Editing Your Life

*Freedom is found through
deliberate subtraction.*

Every item you own demands a piece of you: your money to buy it, your space to store it, your time to maintain it, and your attention to worry about it.

The career you've built can slowly become your prison. Your devices, designed to connect you to everything, can disconnect you from what matters. And the roles you've taken on can trap you into an identity you've outgrown but feel unable to leave.

Much of your story has already been written for you—where you were born, how you look, your natural attributes. You can't control the start of it, and it is true that some stories are fairer than others, but you can control the end.

You are not the author of your life, but you can be the editor.

Great editing, however, prides itself on subtraction, not addition. On discipline via omission.

In a world pushing you toward more possessions and more commitments, your greatest freedom comes from strategic reduction.

This final chapter explores an obvious, yet counterintuitive, truth: to maximize what matters most, you've gotta minimize everything else.

Unhinged Habits

On December 31, 2023, I tried to check into our flight. An error appeared.

The plane is full. You can't add checked bags, it read.

I called Air Transat. They told me that this can happen. That there's nothing they can do. That I should have paid for checked bags in advance when I booked my tickets.

I looked over to Alison. She was sitting on one of our three suitcases trying to zip it closed.

"We're not allowed checked bags."

"What?"

I explained the situation.

"Our two options are to book a new flight for a later date or reduce our luggage to carry-ons," I said.

"Guess I'll only be able to pack tiny outfits."

And that, my friend, is what you call a silver lining.

My wife and I traveled the world with backpacks for six years. Easily a hundred flights between us. We never checked a bag. Then we had a kid. And another. And we accepted that the kind of untethered exploration free from long waits in line at bag drops and luggage carousels was a thing of the past.

Then, last year, the night before leaving for a four-month trip to Nicaragua and Mexico, we weren't allowed to add checked bags. Forced to pack our lives into carry-ons again but this time with a six- and one-year-old, we learned that all that we still need can be packed into a backpack.

Constraints don't diminish your experience; they enhance it.

The less secure you feel, the more you feel you need. Left to your own devices, you'll fill your bags with unnecessary necessities. It's not because you need more stuff; it's because you're scared to be without it. "Shaving down one's pack weight was a process of sloughing off one's fears," wrote Robert Moor in *On Trails*. "Each object a person carries represents a particular fear: of injury, of discomfort, of boredom, of attack."

The Profound Power of Ruthlessly Editing Your Life

At age sixty-one, Meredith Eberhart (a.k.a. the Nimblewill Nomad) started walking and never stopped, covering thirty-four thousand miles in fifteen years. In 2003, he gave his assets to his ex-wife and two sons.

"I tell my friends: every year I've got less and less, and every year, I'm a happier man," said Eberhart. "I just wonder what it's going to be like when I don't have anything. That's the way we come, and that's the way we go. I'm just preparing for that a little in advance, I guess." Much of everything that he owns is in the blue backpack that he carries, no larger than a preschooler's.

Anxiety results from too little confidence in your choices and gets ratcheted up when you introduce a myriad of distracting options.

The reason you're anxious when packing that huge suitcase for a week-long vacation isn't because you're afraid that you'll forget something you need; it's because you don't know what you need in the first place.

Eberhart's extreme. You don't need to follow his lead and replace your toothbrush with a toothpick to shave off weight (seriously). But he is a textbook example that the way to become more resilient is to live with more constraints. To pack a smaller bag.

In 1974, Casio made the first digital watch. It nailed the core features.

A watch needs to tell time and have a timer, alarm, and light. It also needs to be water-resistant and have a long-lasting battery.

For fourteen dollars, Casio nailed it. Their model F-91W is beautiful in its simplicity.

A while back, my wife was gifted an Apple Watch.

We were paddleboarding. She asked me for the time.

"Don't you have your watch on?"

"Yeah, but my phone's out of batteries so it won't pair."

In order for her to tell the time on her $600 watch, it needed to be paired with her $1,000 phone. Both require nightly charging.

I proudly wear a Casio on my wrist as a reminder to do less, better. As a stand for simplicity. A reminder that the problem is rarely complicated, and in order to maximize in areas I care about, I have to pare down everything else to its simplest form. Also, it's nice checking the time without being reminded that I have 217 unread emails. "You can be a whole lot happier if it doesn't take a whole lot to make you happy," said Meredith Eberhart.

Unhinged Habits

One day, my son asked to wear my watch to school.

He lost it.

I wasn't mad. Calvin wanted to feel connected to his dad during the day. Not caring about needless material things is wonderful.

While this chapter does have a minimalist bent, it's not about giving away most things you own (though I wouldn't stop you) or sharing occasionally used items like extension cords with neighbors (again, I wouldn't stop you).

Instead, I'm going to provide frameworks for reducing the brain fog that comes from choice overload, teach you how to optimize your unique attributes, and help you protect your creative energy. Finally, I'll explain why freedom is being able to walk away, even if you choose to stay.

"But Jon, I have two kids and a wife who loves vintage cassette tapes. I can't just throw everything out," my friend said.

Fair point. Not everyone can downsize to a backpack.

When you share your life with others who have their own needs and desires, minimalism looks different. It's not about imposing your preferences. That never works. Instead, lead by example.

My son has thousands of Pokémon cards. I've never suggested he pare down his collection. Instead, I let him watch me donate my cards. For Halloween, we give away my baseball cards alongside candy.

Last fall while sorting cards to give away, he sat down beside me. "Dad, I don't need these ones anymore," he said, adding his own cards to the pile.

Kids learn by watching. Partners too. Your relationship with stuff becomes visible, creating curiosity, not resistance.

Teaching children the difference between wants and needs isn't deprivation. It's a gift that will serve them long after the latest plastic toy breaks.

SMALL HOUSES

Accumulation of possessions indirectly takes over the steering wheel of your life, driving you down ill-advised paths.

Buying more stuff inches you toward "needing" a house with more space, perhaps leading you outside of a city, farther away from loved ones.

The Profound Power of Ruthlessly Editing Your Life

Owning a second car makes it easier to accept a morning commute, wasting hours of precious time a week.

I'm not saying you shouldn't buy a big house or that you don't need a second car. Instead, I'm nudging you to question whether you actually need these things or whether you lazily accepted them as unnecessary necessities. If the latter, have you considered their downstream impacts?

My house isn't large. We have one family area and no basement. As a result, we share space.

Sometimes I hate it. Sometimes I want a place to read in peace and quiet.

I'm lying on the only couch that we own, doing my paper edits of this section. Literally, at this exact moment, Calvin just walked up, lifted my arm, and said, "I'm coming to snuggle even though there isn't much room."

That's the best. The best.

I'm happy that we have a small house.

I don't want to buy a second couch. It's okay that my edits are going to take longer.

I like that we don't quite have enough space.

Small homes help keep families close. How sad must it be to live in a mansion so large that the warmth of your loved ones becomes diffused among the shadows of empty rooms.

We're close to our neighbors. When I close my eyes, I dream of waking up early in another house and looking out cathedral windows at the morning steam rising off the lake, listening to the loon calls in the distance, coffee in hand, French press ready with a refill beside me.

But then I think about last night when I sat on my across-the-street neighbor's porch watching my two boys play hockey on their driveway with three other kids.

I can rent the place on the lake for a week.

My family owns one car. We gave our second to my brother in-law. In its place, I bought a nice bike.

Downstream of that decision, we don't have the expense or worry of a second car. It's also forced me to design a life that exists within a tight perimeter of my house.

Unhinged Habits

On any given weekday, I'll ride a total of about thirty minutes. Extend that out for an eight-month year and that's forty-eight hundred minutes. Over ten years, this one decision has led to forty-eight thousand minutes (or 33.3 consecutive days) of stress-free bonus exercise as opposed to flattening my ass in a car.

Maybe your situation doesn't allow for mostly bike commuting. Maybe your work is far away, or your town's too spread out or you're too rushed and have to drive, or you need all the stuff in every drawer in your house or or or . . .

And maybe all of that is true. But if it is, it's true because it's downstream of previous decisions that you've made. It's possible that those decisions were forced upon you, and there's nothing that you can do about it. Which is totally reasonable. But I know a lot of people who could bike or walk more places. They simply never built the habit. And I know a lot of people that own so much stuff that they feel suffocated. These people are always stressed, always rushed, and not as healthy as they could otherwise be.

The Three Spheres of Intentional Minimalism is a framework encompassing the essential reductions within our physical spaces, mental bandwidth, and personal identities—areas that naturally accumulate as life progresses.

1. **Physical space:** the visible stuff that fills our homes
2. **Mental bandwidth:** the invisible decisions consuming our attention
3. **Identity:** the roles and personas fragmenting our sense of self

Physical minimalism is where most people start because it's tangible. You can literally see the difference when you clear a closet.

But physical decluttering alone isn't enough. I've seen countless friends purge their homes only to remain mentally overwhelmed.

Mental minimalism involves reducing the cognitive burden of constant decisions, notifications, and information overload. When I set my phone to grayscale and removed all nonessential apps from my home screen, it wasn't about being antitechnology. It was about treating my attention as a precious resource.

The most challenging sphere and the one that creates the deepest freedom is identity minimalism. Modern life encourages us to fragment ourselves into specialized roles: professional self, parent self, social media self, community member self.

THE THREE SPHERES OF INTENTIONAL MINIMALISM

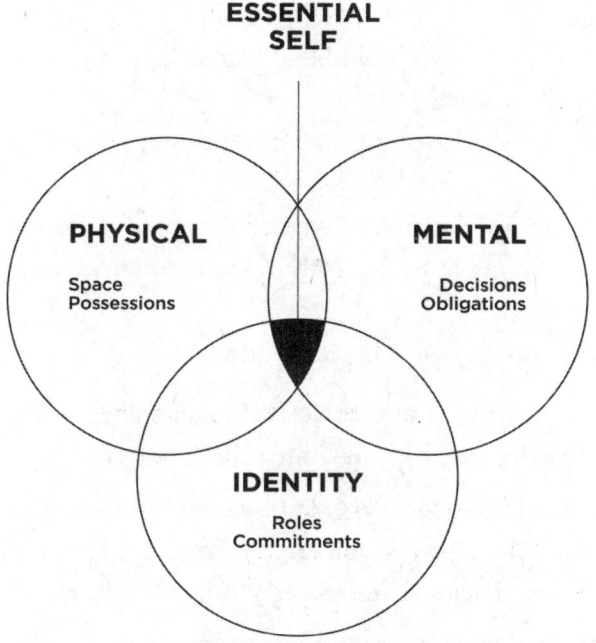

Peeling back the layers of suffocation requires clearing out your home (physical), quieting your mind (mental), and prioritizing the kind of human you want to be (identity). (©Unhinged Habits)

Start small. Try the Ten-Minute Minimization Challenge.

Set a timer for ten minutes and choose one small space (a drawer, a shelf, your phone's home screen).

Ask just one question: "Does this help me maximize what matters?"

Not "might I need this someday?" That's fear talking.

Do this daily for a week. You'll remove dozens of items from your life. More importantly, you'll strengthen your minimization muscle.

Unhinged Habits

The practice scales. From drawers to decisions. From T-shirts to time commitments. From physical clutter to mental noise.

Start with stuff. Graduate to life-changing minimizations.

This minimalist approach extends beyond physical spaces to our digital worlds too.

The average American checks their phone 144 times daily. That's 144 interruptions, 144 task switches. Controlling your device isn't preference; it's protection.

Phones are designed to be addictive. Every app engineered to disrupt, interrupt, and engage you.

Problem is, they're too powerful. I cannot control my phone. My phone controls me.

Perhaps I lack self-control. Maybe that's true. But I know it to be true. So I've stopped trying to resist. Instead, I've redesigned my device to serve me better.

Here's three tips to control your phone:

- **Set your phone to grayscale.** This makes it less addictive. Social media in black and white is hella boring.
- **Turn off all notifications except for text messages.** Give your number only to people you love. Set one rule for after hours at work: emergencies get texts, everything else can wait.
- **Remove all apps from your home screen.** Make your background a photo of somebody or something that you love. When you mindlessly reach for your phone, you'll see that first. Having to swipe to the second screen adds just enough friction to break the trance.

Digital minimalism isn't about becoming a Luddite. It's about treating attention as your most precious resource. Just like with physical possessions, your digital lifestyle shapes your freedom and focus.

Your lifestyle is downstream of your packing habits. The stuff you own ends up owning you. Choose carefully, reassess constantly, and edit mercilessly.

But physical possessions aren't the only things that clutter our lives. Our mental bandwidth faces its own form of overwhelming accumulation: the tyranny of choice. I discovered this in, of all places, Greenland.

GREENLANDIC BEER

Fifty-three people live in Ilimanaq, Greenland. To get there I flew Toronto to Frankfurt to Copenhagen to Kangerlussuaq to Ilulissat, followed by a one-and-a-half-hour boat ride through an ice fjord. The trip took three days.

After some arctic camping, I felt like having a beer. "What kind would you like?" asked Victoria, our server at the lodge.

Stupidity and ignorance are different. Stupidity refers to a lack of general intelligence. Ignorance, on the other hand, is domain specific and refers to a lack of knowledge about a specific thing, issue, or topic.

I'm not stupid. But when it comes to the topic of what beer to order in Greenland, I'm sure as heck ignorant.

"Learning to choose is hard. Learning to choose well is harder. And learning to choose well in a world of unlimited possibilities is harder still, perhaps too hard," wrote the psychologist Barry Schwartz. Americans are given two options for president, but twenty-seven for pasta sauce. Our world is full of needless choices.

Step 1 is to admit your ignorance. It's foolish to deceive yourself into thinking that you have the capacity to make an actual educated decision most of the time. "Gustof is in the kitchen, right?" I asked Victoria. "He seems like the kind of guy who likes beer. Can you ask him what his favorite is and bring me that?"

Step 2 is to find a resident expert.

Step 3 is to ask the right question(s).

And Step 4 is to default to their opinion.

Gustof was our chef for the week. Everything that he made was delicious. Also, he lives in Greenland. I am not a chef, and I do not live in Greenland.

Most of my friends ordered a Carlsberg because that was the only beer that they recognized on the menu. Victoria brought me a Qajaq Tulugaq. It was delicious.

Unhinged Habits

Now you know what beer to buy the next time that you're in Greenland. Here's how the same approach applies to more common purchases.

I wanted to buy a bike. My needs were basic: thirty minutes of riding a day, an occasional thirty-kilometer ride with my dad, and no trail riding or peloton-style cycling. I guess what I'm saying is that my requirements for a bike were that it has wheels that turn.

Websites and bike shops have too many options. No part of me wants to research the differences between sintered, organic, semi-metal, or NAO ceramic brake pads. Within two minutes of googling what to think about when thinking about buying a bike, I entered into the "ain't nobody got time for this shit" phase of my search.

The faster I buy a bike and the fewer cognitive resources I expend in the process the better.

Find an expert: somebody obsessed with the thing you couldn't care less about. In this case, it's my dad. The man loves bikes.

Next, I asked him for the one to two things to look for. Dad told me that tire size and bike weight are most important in addition to a ballpark cost. I then called the first person I could find that sold bikes, told him my guidelines, and said that I wanted to buy a bike.

The salesman sent me a link to a website and asked me to let him know what I wanted. I clicked it. There were about a hundred bikes and customizations to choose from. I texted him back and asked him to pick for me. He's a bike guy. All that I know is that bikes have wheels.

He texted me back with his choice and the link to the page with all of the specs to "go over." I didn't open the link. Instead, I called him to give him my credit card details. He delivered the bike to my house, tuned up and ready to go the following week.

Everything about what I just described is irresponsible and ignorant. It didn't work out. The bike sucked.

But you know what? I'm still happy that I didn't waste time researching the "best bike." The one I got cost $700. Lasted me two seasons. Not as long as a bike should last, of course. But that's fine; it happens.

Most of the time, the outcome of whatever choice you make is good enough for whatever you need or want to achieve. A better product or service accomplishes the goal just the same as something that's good enough,

The Profound Power of Ruthlessly Editing Your Life

and you'll never know the difference anyway. Due diligence, for almost everything that you buy, is a waste of time and energy.

Sometimes you'll end up with a dud. In my case, a bad bike that was sold to me by a jerk. Even in worst case scenarios like this, I still consider what happened a win. (And not just because I got to call Alison and tell her my meaty quads busted the derailer.)

Most people spend ten to twenty hours researching bikes, tricking themselves into thinking that they know enough to make a smart purchase decision. In almost every case, they don't end up with a better product or save anywhere close to the amount of money commensurable to the time they spent. Sometimes what they buy sucks too.

I bought a new bike in an hour. It required three phone calls and one text message exchange. In addition to preserving my mental energy, I also saved somewhere between nine to nineteen hours of time.

Accepting that sometimes what you'll buy will suck is a trade-off you must be willing to make. Because most of the time, it won't. Most of the time what you buy will solve your problem just fine. If you were to do a full accounting, the trade-off of saving so much time on so many purchases, accepting that occasionally, but not often, you'll buy something that sucks, is a fantastic deal.

It seems irresponsible to purposefully make rash purchase decisions based on insubstantial information. I tend to think it's the other way around. I think that it's irresponsible to pretend you know more than you do and waste the most precious resources that you have—your time and energy—in an ill-fated attempt to save a few bucks or get the "best" when all that you need is a bike with wheels that turn.

There will only be a few things you care about. Obsess over them. Spend your time on them. My dad with bikes. Me with junk wax Ken Griffey Jr. baseball cards.

We all have our things.

For everything else, don't even attempt to compare specs or find the best price. Even if you find a better thing cheaper, trading money that you can get back in exchange for time that you've lost forever is a ridiculously foolish endeavor.

HOW TO MAKE GOOD-ENOUGH PURCHASE DECISIONS, FAST

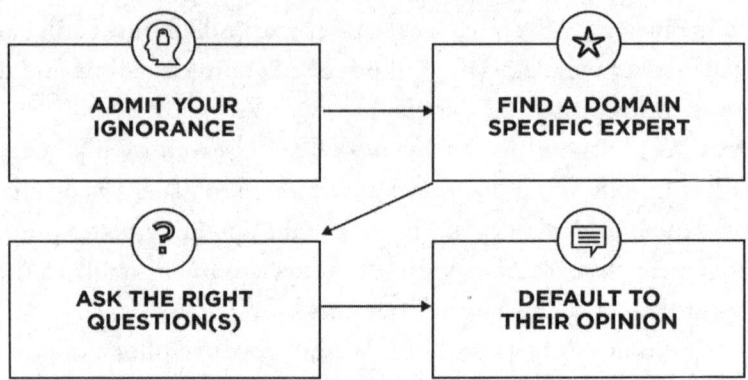

Smart decisions don't require endless research—just honesty about your ignorance, access to expertise, focused questions, and the wisdom to trust informed recommendations. This approach saves time and mental energy and almost always yields good-enough results. (©Unhinged Habits)

The happiest and most successful people that I know are decisive. They decide, move forward, and live with the consequences while others live in a self-imposed imprisonment, overwhelmed by their own indecision, complaining that there aren't enough hours in the day.

By minimizing the mental load of choices, you free up cognitive resources for the things that warrant your full attention.

While decision simplification frees your mind from trivial choices, there's another benefit to minimalism that became apparent to me when I was lying in a single bed in the Albanian Alps.

ALBANIAN KOFFE

Alison and I celebrated our third wedding anniversary by sleeping in separate single beds.

After two days of Balkan travel, we completed the thirteen-mile trek across the Accursed Mountains in the Albanian Alps. The trek was tough, but we took our time, enjoying a *koffe* in each *kafe* along the way, filling our bottles with the spring water that flowed out of the mountains.

Tired and with achy knees, we arrived at the Sphella Guesthouse in the village of Theth, our home for the night.

"Goodman, Jonathan. Are you a Good Man?" the man asked.

"Of course. My family is full of Good Men," I replied.

Our Albanian host (average height, slim, and with a thick black beard) appeared satisfied with my outrageously witty response and showed us upstairs to our room.

Inside the stone guesthouse we see three single beds and a door leading to our private toilet—a luxury in these parts. The shower is cold, so we wash off the dirt and the sweat from the hike but don't linger.

To some reading, I expect that this adventure I've briefly described sounds like a dream. The dream. Wanderlust.

For others, it sounds miserable. Travel like this is not the type of thing you'll see a twenty-one-year-old lifestyle influencer who knows nothing of the world bragging about doing.

Joy is not an objective emotion. It is best felt when preceded by hardship. Experience enriches. The best lives are the ones that include struggle and strife. In order to love, you must hurt. In order to feel pleasure, you must feel pain. In order to relax, you must first toil. This necessary juxtaposition in experience is often missing in our otherwise too-easy lives.

We wake in separate beds. I look over to Alison and say I love you. I crack my back, she pops her hip. We both pee. Then walk downstairs for breakfast.

"Everything is homemade," thick-beard said. "The butter, the eggs, the honey, and even the wine you drank last night are made here."

I was especially thankful for the honey because the horrible koffe needed two heaping spoonfuls to be palatable. After a few sips, I could think my morning thoughts.

Here's what they were:

I told Alison how special it was that we don't spend our time thinking about most things.

That I'm happy we don't get consumed by celebrity gossip, political nonsense, or the financial markets. That it's okay neither of us have any idea what new movies are coming out or what reality TV show is trending.

But, I said to her, it's not just that we don't know about these things. It's deeper than that. We don't even think about thinking about them.

Until the morning after a three-day adventure in the north of Albania, I'd never realized that, for better or for worse, the apparent obsessions of so many others are foreign constructs to us.

This is neither good nor bad. I'm not writing this to appear more noble or evolved. Perhaps some thinking on politics or the financial markets would serve me well. I don't know if not thinking about this stuff is a good thing or not. But I certainly don't feel like I'm missing out. And I've never seen a single person become happier by spending more time following politics or the news. So maybe, just maybe, stripping our lives of these distractions allows us to live more fully.

This realization connects to a critical question: What if our entire approach to personal development is backward? What if, instead of becoming well-rounded, we should focus on becoming exceptional at just one thing? On depth, not breadth? On obsession?

ANIMAL SCHOOL

A rabbit, a fish, a bird, a squirrel, and a bunch of other animals start a school.

Arguments began when they sat down to write the curriculum. Rabbit wanted running to be included; fish wanted swimming; bird wanted flying; and squirrel insisted that there be a class on advanced tree-climbing techniques.

To appease the group, a well-intentioned mediator added each animal's specialty into the programming. Then they made the mistake of insisting that all animals take all classes.

The rabbit cruised through the running lessons, but the instructors said that it was good intellectual and emotional discipline for it to also take flying lessons. So the rabbit did what it was told, climbed up onto a ledge, and jumped off, flapping its wings just as it was taught.

The poor thing fell and broke a leg. It could never fly, but now it can't run well either and so instead of getting an A+ in running, it got a C.

The Profound Power of Ruthlessly Editing Your Life

The fish had a similar experience. It did well in the swimming class. But then it was time for tree climbing . . . well, you can guess how that went. The teachers gave the fish a D in climbing (because the fish asserted itself), but it had become dehydrated in the process and lost all motivation to swim, receiving a C-. At the end of the year, the valedictorian of the class was an intellectually disabled salamander.

English came naturally to me in high school. All A's. Math, on the other hand, was a struggle. Solid C's. In order for me to get accepted into a good university, my average needed to improve. My parents got me a math tutor.

What happened next was a real-life version of an animal school. Math, a subject I showed no natural aptitude for, became the focus. English got ignored because I was already good at it. The strategy worked. I got into a good university.

But does any of this make sense?

I don't think so.

I should have had an English tutor, perhaps a writing coach.

You may be a genius. You may be a great writer. But you can't get into a university unless you can also figure out the cos angle of a triangle. That makes no sense.

There are compelling examples of people who have followed their singular strength, resisting the pressure to be well-rounded.

Like Temple Grandin, the animal science professor who revolutionized livestock handling by leaning into her autism rather than trying to overcome it. While others pressured her to develop more "normal" social skills, she doubled down on her singular ability to think visually like animals.

Or Colonel John Boyd, the Air Force officer who obsessively focused on aerial combat theory despite pressure to become a well-rounded military leader. He refused promotions that would have diversified his responsibilities and instead developed just one idea: the OODA loop (Observe, Orient, Decide, Act).

These aren't just success stories. They're rebellions against the "well-rounded" myth we're brought up to believe.

When we're young, external validations in the way of grades, averaged out across a wide array of opposing aptitudes, is what you're judged on. But then you get into the real world, and it doesn't matter if a rabbit can

Unhinged Habits

fly; because the rabbit's hella fast. And fish don't need to climb trees; they swim.

You have a thing. A thing that comes natural to you. A thing that you just seem to *get*. Where you wonder why, even if it's hard, you have boundless energy for it. A thing that makes sense to you in a way that disables you from having conversations with most others about it because it's so clear to you and foreign to them.

Like Grandin and Boyd, I eventually found my singular focus—writing. I don't know why it's writing. Writing is hard. Most nights I go to bed and hate what I wrote and feel like a failure. But then I'm excited to write again the next day.

There's nothing else that causes me the same exquisite combination of anger, frustration, and elation that writing does. It's never burned me out. No matter how hard I've struggled with it, it's never burned me out. That's how I know that it's my thing.

Once you find your thing, obsess over it. Put an absurd amount of effort into it. Accept the trade-off that nothing you could work on matters as much as it does. Pursue mastery.

I write every morning for two hours before my family wakes up. I don't like to wake up early. But early morning is when my brain works best. So I wake up early.

Waking up early is a constraint (like packing a small backpack) that has downstream effects on the rest of my life.

Because I wake up early, I go to bed early. I don't drink alcohol because it wrecks my sleep. I rarely accept invites to social events at night or attend concerts because they end late.

I'd love to see more live music. But I'm not willing to sacrifice my writing for it. I've also turned down advisory board invitations. In order to maximize, you must minimize. Identify the trade-offs. Accept them gladly.

I don't read a lot of books on writing, but I do read a lot. And everything I read, I read with the goal of improving my writing. I wish that I could read for pure pleasure. I'm simply unable.

Whether it's fiction or nonfiction, I'm studying. The title of the introduction of my previous book *The Obvious Choice* is "Business Was Great,

The Profound Power of Ruthlessly Editing Your Life

Once." The first line of *Elantris* by Brandon Sanderson is "Elantris was beautiful, once."

Everybody's got a thing. Most never pursue it fully and therefore never thrive. "Bring up your average," you're told. Fly, if you're a fast runner. Climb, if you're a good swimmer.

Being average isn't fun. If you follow that path, your energy will ebb and flow: feeling motivated for brief periods before burning out again.

Burning out isn't the result of working too hard for too long. It happens when you work on the wrong things or too many things.

You've got your thing. You know what it is. The more you design everything else you do to maximize it, the better. The less of everything else, the better.

There's nuance to this conversation though. A but.

The corollary to the animal school parable is that mastery over one thing is great and fun and absolutely something to go after. But if you want to be conventionally successful with it, your thing needs to be supported by mediocre-to-just-okay levels in what I call "Leapfrog Skills"—a concept I discuss at length in my previous book.

The five biggest Leapfrog Skills are:

1. Business writing
2. Behavioral psychology
3. Conversation
4. Sales
5. Wealth management

Basic arithmetic undoubtedly matters. But beyond a certain point, if a person isn't going to go into a career that requires complex mathematics, its importance falls off a cliff.

Finding your thing and focusing on it is liberating. But there's another paradox to explore: sometimes giving away what you've built creates even more space for mastery.

TZEDAKAH

There's a principle in Christianity that I like, which basically says that we never own anything.

All that exists is a loan from God. Everything was God's property before we arrived and will be returned to him after we die.

I like this because it puts into better perspective the concept of ownership. Getting more isn't the point. Being more useful and enjoying more of what we have during our short time on this earth is the point. Which, in turn, frees us from the burden of ownership.

Tzedakah is a Hebrew word meaning "righteousness." While charity is generally understood as the act of giving money, tzedakah differs in that it is an obligation to do what is right.

Giving isn't just about financial gain or karma. It's about enabling us to keep doing the work that we love with people that we enjoy being around. What I've found holds people back from giving is a notion of whether it's fair or not.

The principle of tzedakah works for people at every resource level, not just for those with businesses or significant financial assets. In fact, those with the least often understand this principle most deeply.

Consider James, a retiree living on a fixed income in a modest apartment. For years, he taught carpentry at a local high school. Now, every Tuesday and Thursday, he repairs furniture at a community center. He could charge for these services, but he chooses to offer them freely.

What James receives in return isn't financial. It's purpose, community, and the knowledge that his skills aren't going to waste.

Elena's another example. She works as a health aide. Her income is limited and her schedule's demanding. Twice a month she hosts a "skills exchange potluck" in the common room of her building. People bring food and teach each other practical skills like conversational Spanish or how to fix a leaky faucet.

"I realized I couldn't afford the time or money for classes in all the things I wanted to learn. But, collectively, we already know so much," she said.

The Profound Power of Ruthlessly Editing Your Life

Elena's gifts: organization and initiative. She created abundance where scarcity existed before.

Here are six currencies you can give away beyond money:

- **Attention:** Truly listening to someone
- **Knowledge:** Sharing what you know
- **Time:** Showing up consistently for someone or something
- **Space:** Opening your home, however humble
- **Connections:** Introducing people who might help each other
- **Encouragement:** Offering genuine support when someone is struggling

The paradox of giving applies to all these currencies.

There are a lot of ways to measure wealth. Money is one. Another is how much time and energy you are able to commit to the thing that brings you the most joy. *Your Thing.* I tend to think that once you get to the point of "enough" with money, the second is far more valuable to maximize.

Again, my thing is writing.

In order to write interesting things, you have to also live an interesting life. To do stuff outside of writing so that you have stuff to write about. For me, this includes operating businesses and going on adventures. In order to focus on my writing and have time to go on adventures, I gave away 50 percent of the two biggest businesses that I own—my mentorship and my software platform.

I started both, funded them, took all of the risk, and then gave away half of each to somebody else who operates them as their own business.

My business owner friends laughed at me. "Why didn't you just hire a CEO?" "You could have sold the thing and walked away." "You got hosed on that deal," one even told me. They thought I didn't get it. I knew they didn't.

Whether or not something is fair financially is only part of the conversation. My goal is to maximize the quality of my output while never missing a minute with my wife and kids.

Unhinged Habits

So what if somebody else wins big and I could have possibly gotten a better deal? As long as the deal that I got was good and the deal that they got was good, that's cool.

The Giving Paradox: Give more, get more.

You can eat a big piece of a small pie or expand the pie and share it with friends. What I've found is that the more pie that you share, the bigger it grows.

My mentorship was doing $300,000 in revenue a year (about $200k in profit) when I handed it off. Today, three years later, it makes more than $5 million a year ($3.2M profit). It's thriving because running a business like that is "the thing" for the person running it, same as writing is mine.

Handing off the software platform is newer. Its benefits can't be measured yet.

Both cases were a great deal for the other person. Me too. What I gave away had real and tangible value. What I got in return went beyond money. I got more time, less stress, and more freedom to pursue mastery.

People in competitive fields like law, medicine, finance, and tech sometimes push back on me. The pressure to excel is intense. But even here—especially here—strategic minimization creates advantage.

Look at the unspoken assumptions in your field. The "must-dos" that everyone accepts as gospel.

Most aren't universal or mandatory.

Find the true top performers. They're not doing everything. They've identified the few vital things that matter and become exceptional at those while merely appearing competent at the rest.

My mentorship story isn't unique. It's a pattern.

The business didn't grow to $5 million despite my stepping away. It grew because of it. Because I stopped being the bottleneck. Because I focused on what I do best and let someone else focus on what they do best.

Specialization isn't limitation. It's leverage.

Like a laser, the more focused your energy, the more impact you create.

Maimonides, widely considered the most influential Torah scholar of the Middle Ages, described eight ascending degrees of tzedakah. At the top, the step that brings you closest "closest to heaven" is:

"The person who helps another to become self-supporting by a gift or a loan or by finding employment for the recipient."

This sentiment crosses borders and religions. The most important sentiments always do.

In Chinese philosophy: "Give a man a fish and you feed him for a day. Teach him how to fish and you feed him for a lifetime."

The Islamic practice of *sadaqah* suggests its followers "guide the blind" and "support the weak with the strength of your arms."

The giving paradox of giving more to get more is said in Judaism, Christianity, and Islam to bring you closer to heaven, God, and Allah respectively.

Ironic that the things that bring us closer to divinity also tend to improve our quality of life here on earth. Maybe all this talk of a greater power is just a handy way of nudging you toward being a better person for yourself and others. Kind of like Santa Claus, but for adults.

If an aspect of what you do is holding you back, give it away without care or consideration of whether it's a fair financial trade. What you'll gain goes far beyond money. And the most striking aspect is that it very often leads to more money too.

This principle of strategic release extends beyond business and into every area of your life. The ultimate freedom comes from maintaining your ability to walk away.

REDUCING YOUR WALKING COSTS

Remember Andrew from earlier? My one true friend who embarked on his "month of yes" and found love? Years later, he had become good at a job he no longer wanted to do.

The forces keeping him there were strong. It started with the sunk cost associated with his costly degree, not to mention seven years of university. Then he leased an expensive truck, bought a home with his wife, and leased a second expensive SUV. All these *things*.

"I'm feeling stuck," he told me.

Unhinged Habits

He said that he hates his work. That he sees his two children a lot but he's never *there* with them. When his phone often buzzes after hours, he feels that he has to check it.

"Whoa, that's a nice collection," I said, pointing to his liquor cabinet.

"I started drinking whiskey at night to relax. Just one, most nights. Sometimes two . . . or three."

After getting his master's degree, my friend got a job. The business grew. He became its number two. Days turned into months, which turned into one year, then two, and now twelve. For almost the entire time he's dreamed of doing something else. But he's worked hard to get to where he is. Leaving feels like too much to lose. So he's stayed.

"Why don't you quit?"

"We can't afford it."

My friend and his wife make plenty. And yet he feels stuck. That's because, as his income rose, so did his status in his community, his ego as a provider, the perceived standing he had within his extended family, and, of course, the things that he owned.

Which brings us to the point our journey has been headed toward all along.

FREEDOM

Two years after our conversation, something changed for my friend. On March 18, 2025, he sent me a voice note.

"So, I need your help.

"I've left my house for the last time. And I've got a car packed full of all our personal shit. Before we head down tomorrow morning to start our journey to Austin, it's my last night here in Thornhill. And I don't know what to do. I don't know where to go. Listen, I'm going to sleep at my in-laws. I know that. But where do I go for dinner? Who do I call? I can kinda do anything. And you know what? It's freeing, but it's scary."

We spoke that night. I made up an absurdly elaborate story about an underground cult of pigeons led by one named Reginald who were conspiring to keep him in Toronto—anything to distract him from the weight of the moment.

The Profound Power of Ruthlessly Editing Your Life

But a few days later, as his car pointed toward Austin and away from everything familiar, I felt feelings. This was a guy I'd known since I was eight. I'm going to miss him. Selfishly, I didn't want him to leave. And yet I felt profound joy that after all these years of feeling trapped, he was finally walking away—proving he could.

I texted him: "Love the adventure you're on, moving your family. Am going to miss the heck out of you. Super happy for you."

"Likewise brother," he replied. Then he added, "I fully expect a visit from the Goodmans."

His story illustrated something essential: freedom isn't being able to live out your days on a beach or buy private planes. It's simpler than that.

Freedom is optionality.

Freedom is providing yourself an opportunity to fail.

Freedom is the ability to do what you want, when you want, with whom you want. Because if you're not working on your ideal day, chances are you're working on someone else's.

The fewer options you have, the less freedom you've earned, and the more stuck you'll feel. You might never decide to exercise your options. That's fine. Stay with your work, buy the costly car, join the bourgie country club. Wonderful. But accept those things only under one condition: that sticking with them is your decision, not one imposed upon you. Freedom is knowing that you can move on, even if you decide not to. Freedom is control. If you want to be free, you must keep your walking costs low.

Walking costs come in three forms:

1. **Financial costs:** Debt, recurring payments, lifestyle inflation that requires your current income.
2. **Relational costs:** Obligations, social expectations, commitments to energy vampires.
3. **Identity costs:** Titles, status, and self-perceptions you've invested in but no longer serve you.

For each category, ask, *What's one thing I could eliminate that would increase my freedom without reducing what truly matters?*

Unhinged Habits

The highest walking costs are usually the ones you've convinced yourself are nonnegotiable. My friend has skills, savings, and spousal support. What he views as prohibitive walking costs are, to any outsider, an illusion.

"Quit your job," you tell your cousin, though you're secretly burned the heck out yourself. "Cut off that abusive relative," you say, thinking about your own crazy aunt. "Sell that bad investment. Stop throwing good money after bad," you advise, still holding on to your bag of meme coins that you bought at the height of whatever idiotic hysteria you were bored enough to pay attention to. We humans are skilled at counseling others with logic while simultaneously drowning in our own emotions and fabrications.

Are you really as tied down as you think that you are?

For many of us, we've been working hard to get to some endpoint—the pot of gold at the end of the rainbow. And if we quit, it feels like all our work up until now has been for nothing.

But is that true?

You might be thinking right now that you can't afford it. What is it? I've no idea. But you're worried that whatever it is, you can't afford it.

Well, have you done the math?

I'm not advising you to quit. And I'm not advising you to stay. I'm just hoping that you'll consider what you're actually scared of and whether it's justified or not. Then, if it serves you, make some changes that, with the benefit of hindsight, will appear obvious.

If you're worried about what "they" are going to think, well, who are *they* and do *they* matter?

A while back I called a mentor to talk over some complicated things with my business. After an hour of going through all the details, I waited for his advice.

"Jon, it doesn't matter," he said.

I wrote that down. *It doesn't matter.* Got it. Then I looked up at him. He chuckled to himself and shared an analogy he heard from the pastor Steven Furtick.

The Profound Power of Ruthlessly Editing Your Life

"You're stressed out because you have this feed. And everything on it is the same size. Because it's the same size, you think it carries the same weight. You're living in a state of stress because you haven't learned how to weigh it out. You haven't learned that 99.9993 percent of what's keeping you up at night *doesn't matter*. And that's why you don't have energy left for the few things that do," he said.

Then, for good measure, he added the kicker:

"How do you ever expect to find peace when your life is split into so many pieces?"

You have four thousand weeks; 960 months. That's an insane framing. Life is too short to be anxious. Anxious about paying off the things you don't need but somehow own. Anxious about maintaining relationships that no longer serve you. And anxious about doing work you're good at but no longer want to be doing.

When I look down at my wrist now, I see another fourteen-dollar Casio. The third one this year.

Calvin keeps asking to wear it to school. I keep saying yes. He keeps losing them.

Some losses simply don't matter. That's the final message I want to leave you with. To carry less physical, mental, and emotional weight. Transformational change is hard. Adopting the habits of letting go of everything that you don't need, even if it looks unhinged to others, takes courage.

You know, I was looking at the word *anxious* just now and noticed that in the middle of the word is the letter *i* and at the end is *-us*.

And I was thinking about why we work so hard. That too often the work begins to feel like the point. Or why we buy the stuff we buy. That too often the stuff we buy begins to feel like the point. Or why we let others' perceptions guide us on how to show up in the world. That too often satisfying our own egos feels like the point. And how all any of this does is make us anxious.

And then I noticed the solution staring me in the face.

When you let yourself become owned by your belongings, your work, or your ego, you become suffocated by your own selfishness. Stuck in the middle. Obsessing over things that don't matter. Only thinking about the *i*. About yourself.

The way to become less anxious is to go from *i* to *-us*. *It's right there in the word*. By minimizing needless choices, unnecessary necessities, and your attachment to empty extravagances, you maximize your time, your energy, and your money to share with others. That's how you take control. And when you're in control, you become free.

Let's now end our story where it began.

CHAPTER 8 SUMMARY

- **Focus obsessively on your "thing."** Instead of pursuing well-roundedness, identify what naturally energizes you and design your life to maximize it, accepting the necessary trade-offs this focus requires.

- **Declutter your possessions, decisions, and commitments.** Physical objects, constant choices, and too many roles all compete for your limited energy. Start with clearing visible spaces, then simplify your daily decisions, and finally release identities that no longer serve you.

- **Outsource low-stakes decisions to experts.** Admit your ignorance in most domains, find relevant experts, ask the right questions, and default to their opinion rather than wasting cognitive resources on choices that don't deserve your attention.

- **Keep your walking costs low.** True freedom isn't wealth or status. True freedom is having options—the ability to change course when needed. Maintain this freedom by minimizing financial obligations, relational burdens, and identifying attachments that silently trap you.

THE HALF-FULL CUP

November 2, 2024

Alison made it to her second trimester. She's not great but feeling better.

The next day, she went to get an imaging ultrasound and sent me a text message soon after: "We could hardly see the heartbeat. Baby wouldn't stop moving! ♥"

So that's why, this morning, at 6:00 a.m., on Saturday, November 2, I'm sitting in my cold office crying—finally letting myself feel all of the emotions I've been holding in for the past month and a half while I was trying to be strong for my family, for my boys, and mostly, for Alison, who just taught me what being strong really means. Writing up our story. Grateful our cup was only half full because we just needed every ounce of that space.

Then, on March 21, 2025, our neighbor, Eliane, sent us a message:

"I had an appointment with my surgeon, and he said that I am free of cancer now. I will keep doing the immunotherapy until December, and I will be done with all of this cancer thing. Thank you so much guys for all your help and support. Love you."

And finally, on May 13, Jasmine was born.

Books are tasked impossibly with making order out of disorder and chaos. But books are never the truth. The truth is chaos.

Happiness, I've discovered, isn't a destination—it's a direction. An iterative process. A search with no end that needs sorrow to feel the joy, pain to feel the pleasure, and work to relax.

The world hasn't changed much in the past thirteen years where I've gotten married, had three children, and traveled for a total of almost two thousand days. If anything, it's gone farther off the rails. But I've changed. I no longer experience it in the same way.

To paraphrase David Brooks, freedom isn't an ocean to explore. Freedom is a river to cross so that you can make a home somewhere on the other side—and fully commit to someone and something.

The best use of life is figuring out a way to spend as much of it as possible with the people you love. Like buying a house a six-minute-forty-nine-second walk from your parents.

When we first moved in, I set my backpack down into the corner of our walk-in closet, hung my three Merino wool T-shirts, looked at Alison, and said, "I guess we should buy a fork."

Over a decade of exploration has led me back to where it started, appreciative and grateful in a way that would have otherwise been impossible. I've traveled a long way in search of what I needed and returned home to find it.

Jonathan Goodman
Toronto, Canada

ACKNOWLEDGMENTS

Are we doing this again already? Wow, guess so. Okay, I just checked, and the acknowledgments for my last book were only submitted a year ago.

This book took a lot of hours to write. While it was written quickly, it was not written fast. Which meant that I needed a lot of focused time to plug away.

In the tzedakah section of this book, I talk about giving more to get more. My first thank-you goes out to the teams that operate and work across my companies. In giving you control and a big part of the upside, I've gotten the space to dive in and write, knowing you're taking incredible care of our customers, our team, and our bottom line.

In no particular order, thanks to Drea Maxwell, Jason Maxwell, Amber Bonem, Misty Overstreet, Brad Overstreet, Alex Harriman, Alina Parades, Allan Misner, Carin Timskog, Carmelina Karas, Christa Baker, Jeff Dalzell, Jon Vlahogiannakos, Josué Cid, Kaylee Bennett, Kristine Michaud, Malcolm McNeill, Patrick Ryan II, Reynaldo Reyna, and Sofija Janeva.

Like many authors, I love to write but don't love figuring out how to talk about what I write on social media. A special thank-you to Stanley Goldberg for showing up every few months with a video camera, asking me questions, filming the whole thing, and keeping my online platform going so that I can focus. And also a thank-you to Drex for the beautiful illustrations both here and on my social media.

Not only would this book have taken longer, but it wouldn't be anywhere near as good without the support of my fabulous publishing team. Jaidree Braddix, thanks for being an incredible thought partner/friend/agent. Tim Burgard, you have a way of staying out of the way and letting me cook while popping in exactly when I need it. Thanks for not taking over the project but also being willing to suggest changes. And to Matt,

Acknowledgments

Sicily, and the rest of the publishing and marketing teams at HarperCollins Leadership, thank you for the support.

Next, a big thank-you to a few of the wonderful people who gave permission to have their stories told. Eliane, I'm so happy you're cancer-free! You're a fighter and an inspiration. And Andrew (whose real name is also Jon, but that would've been confusing in the book so I had to change it), you told me that you're honored to have your story included. That you hope it helps others shed light on the possibilities this world gives us and the opportunities we make for ourselves. My friend, the honor's all mine. And I hope so too. Thank you for leading the way.

Finally, Alison, this book is for you. I love you.

ABOUT THE AUTHOR

Jonathan Goodman has spent thirteen winters exploring the world—first solo, then with his wife, and now with their three children—challenging educational conventions while building multimillion-dollar businesses. Featured in *The New York Times*, *Men's Health*, *Forbes*, *Robb Report*, *Entrepreneur*, and *Inc.*, Jon proves that you don't have to choose between professional success, meaningful relationships, and fulfilling adventure. He is based in Toronto.